THIS BOOK BELONGS TO:

Name _____

Address _____

City _____

State _____

Telephone Number _____

A WRITING BOOK

English in Everyday Life

Tina Kasloff Carver

Sandra Douglas Fotinos

Christie Kay Olson

Cross-Cultural Communications Collaborative

ALEMANY PRESS
PRENTICE HALL REGENTS, Engelwood Cliffs, NJ 07632

Library of Congress Cataloging in Publication Data

Carver, Tina Kasloff, (date)
    A writing book.

    Includes index.
        1. English language—Text-books for foreigners.
2. English language—Composition and exercises.
I. Fotinos, Sandra Douglas, 1940-   . II. Olson,
Christie Kay.   III. Title.
PE1128.C43   428.2'4   81-19176
ISBN 0-13-970129-X   AACR2

. . . dedicated to the immigrants in our families
who, coming to a new country, had to learn
a new language and a new life

© 1982 by Prentice Hall Regents
Prentice-Hall, Inc.
A Paramount Communications Company
Englewood Cliffs, New Jersey 07632

Printed in the United States of America

10   9

ISBN 0-13-970129-X

Editorial/production supervision by Virginia Rubens
Interior design by Judy Winthrop
Page layout by Margaret Mary Finnerty
Cover design by Barbara Shelly/20/20 Services Inc.
Manufacturing buyer: Harry P. Baisley

Prentice-Hall International (UK) Limited, *London*
Prentice-Hall of Australia Pty. Limited, *Sydney*
Prentice-Hall Canada Inc., *Toronto*
Prentice-Hall Hispanoamericana, S.A., *Mexico*
Prentice-Hall of India Private Limited, *New Delhi*
Prentice-Hall of Japan, Inc., *Tokyo*
Simon & Schuster Asia Pte. Ltd., *Singapore*
Editora Prentice-Hall do Brasil, Ltda., *Rio de Janeiro*

Contents

Preface

Most ESL students are confronted with English writing tasks in their everyday lives before they are ready to handle them. Whether they need to fill out a driver's license application or write an absence note for a child in school or open a bank account, the problem is still the same—the need to write in English arises before they know how to do it.

The purpose of this book is to show students how to meet their everyday writing needs, by introducing them to a wide variety of writing tasks, and to the conventions associated with each task. Most everyday writing tasks are highly conventional, and students do not need to know a lot of English grammar in order to follow these conventions. However, some degree of literacy in English is necessary before beginning these tasks.

In the first pages of the book we have included many exercises in printing and handwriting. These pages address the diverse needs of ESL students at different levels and of different language backgrounds: practicing basic formation of individual letters of the alphabet, reviewing "legible handwriting," and pointing out real-life instances where handwriting and printing are used.

Succeeding chapters give concrete practice in the many ways writing must be used in our culture: lists, forms, checks, notes, business letters, cards, telegrams, newspaper announcements and diaries. The information provided will be useful for students of all levels of ESL ability, but some writing tasks are too difficult for students with very limited proficiency in English. Therefore, we have broken down the difficult writing tasks into more manageable segments, and provided exercises based on models to guide the students. Thus, even students with a limited background in English will be able to complete the tasks successfully. Other exercises (*Write Your Own* and *Other Vocabulary*) lead intermediate and advanced students to create both practical and personal writing that is really their own, such as a report of a car accident or a request for a college application.

Some of the chapters are organized on a structural basis, such as **Notes, Business Letters** and **Announcements.** Others are organized thematically, such as **Employment, Traveling** and **Consumer Needs.** The table of contents offers one possible way of organizing the writing tasks, but many other sequences are equally viable. For example, a teacher using a structural approach might want to group all the telegrams or U.S. government forms into a single writing unit. On the other hand, a teacher using a thematic approach could group several pages from different chapters into a writing unit on birthdays, using the pages **Printed Fill-In Invitations, Birthday Cards, Thank You for a Gift,** and **Thank You for Remembering.** The index includes a number of possible additional groupings.

Long after the class is over, the book can continue to serve as a reference for the students. For instance, students might not apply for a job while they are enrolled in the ESL class. However, if they do later, they will already have their résumé and cover letter to use, as well as completed tax forms and an employment application to which they can refer.

The writing tasks we have included reflect the problems and interests of our students, whom we would like to thank for showing us the need for this book, and for testing it through its many revisions.

We would also like to thank the following people for their help:
- Sam Thompson, our design consultant and friend;
- Linda Moussouris, our Cross-Comm colleague;
- Kien Le, Ed Fice, George Hoffman, Barbara Dalba, Jane Thiefels, Paula Cordeiro and Allan Hislop at Northern Essex Community College;
- Sheila Cox at Blue Cross and Blue Shield of Massachusetts, Inc.;
- The International FOCUS group at Park Street Church, Boston;
- The staff at the Instituto Cultural Dominico Americano.

Finally, we would like to thank our families: Ruth Kasloff, Jeffrey, Brian, and Daniel Carver; Hertha Douglas, Xenofon, Christina, Elizabeth and Paul Fotinos; and Ivan and Alice Olson; and Pam Kirshen, our editor at Prentice-Hall, who believed in the project from the start, and whose unwavering confidence encouraged us throughout the long process of completing it.

To the Student

A WRITING BOOK: *English in Everyday Life* has three objectives:

1. To give you practice with common writing tasks in English.
2. To increase your vocabulary for these writing tasks.
3. To give you handwriting practice.

There are four kinds of exercises in the book:

1 WITH YOUR CLASS:

Exercises in vocabulary, reading, and discussion for the writing tasks. In these exercises, you will share information from your personal experiences with the class.

2 ON THE BOARD:

These exercises ask you to write additional vocabulary and charts on the board with your class. Always copy these board exercises in your notebook.

3 WRITE YOUR OWN:

These exercises give you practice writing by yourself, using the models in the book. The exercises include handwriting, filling in forms, writing cards, notes, letters, telegrams, and lists.

4 WITH YOUR PARTNER:

In these exercises, you work with a partner, or sometimes with a small group, on a writing task such as cosigning a loan, writing letters and invitations, and composing classified ads.

Do	Don't
• Do use your dictionary.	• Don't worry if you don't remember all the vocabulary.
• Do keep a notebook.	
• Do share your knowledge with your class.	• Don't guess. Don't fill in the pages until you have discussed them with the class.
• Do ask questions if you don't understand.	• Don't rush.
• Do ask your classmates for help.	• Don't worry if some of the exercises are too hard or too easy for you. Everyday writing tasks include many different degrees of difficulty. Do what you can do and what you need to do.
• Do recopy journals, notes, and letters in your notebook to practice punctuation.	

Printing
and
Handwriting

Teacher's Notes

Student Objectives:
- *to review the principles of printing and handwriting*
- *to practice writing signatures, time and dates*

Sequence

1 Tell the students not to write anything until the class has discussed the page.

2 Preview this chapter by having students fill in the identification form on page i. Use this writing sample as a means of evaluating students' handwriting/printing skills and preferences.

3 Explain to the class that English is written using the Roman alphabet, which was created by the Romans around 1000 B.C. Have students demonstrate on the blackboard the writing systems used in their native languages.

4 Not all students may need to review the basic principles of handwriting and printing. These pages can be assigned individually.

   a Preview the pages that ask students to trace letters by demonstrating on the board how to follow the arrows to form a letter correctly. The sequence of strokes you use or suggest may be slightly different from that shown. It may be interesting for the students to write their letters on the board and explain step by step the strokes they use.

   b Preview the pages that ask students to attach letters or write different-sized letters together by reading the instructions together and demonstrating the principles on the blackboard.

5 The rest of the chapter—**Printing Your Name, Writing Your Signature, Writing Legibly, Time Abbreviations,** and **Writing Dates**—can be completed as a class.

Printing Upper-Case Letters
(Capital Letters)

1 WRITE YOUR OWN: Trace the Capital Letters

Follow the arrows to trace these printed capital letters.

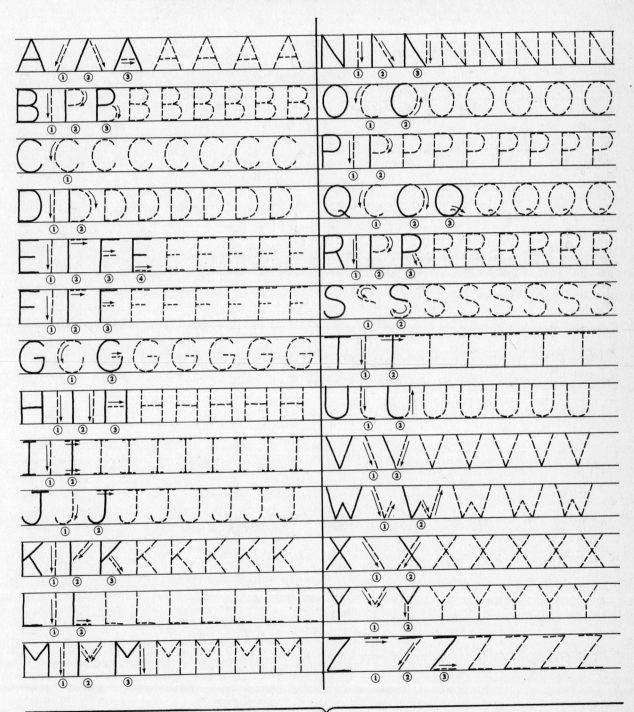

Printing Lower-Case Letters
(Small Letters)

1 WRITE YOUR OWN: Trace the Lower-Case Letters

Follow the arrows to trace the printed lower-case letters.

Tracing practice rows for lower-case letters: a, b, c, d, e, f, g, h, i, j, k, l, m, n, o, p, q, r, s, t, u, v, w, x, y, z

Size of Upper- and Lower-Case Letters (Printing)

1   WITH YOUR CLASS: Different-Sized Letters

Look at the chart below. All upper-case letters fill the space between two lines: A . There are four sizes of lower-case letters. Some fill the space between the lines: b . Some fill only half the space: c . Some fill half the space and extend below the line: g . One letter fills three-quarters of the space: t . Identify the size of each lower-case letter with your class.

2   WRITE YOUR OWN: Upper- and Lower-Case Alphabet

Copy the alphabet below. Print each letter the correct size.

Aa	Jj
Bb	Kk
Cc	Ll
Dd	Mm
Ee	Nn
Ff	Oo
Gg	Pp
Hh	Qq
Ii	Rr

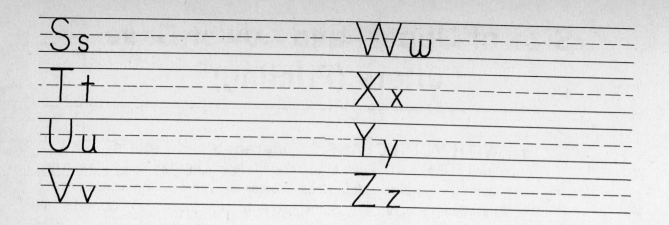

Ss   Ww

Tt   Xx

Uu   Yy

Vv   Zz

Printing Your Name

In English there are usually three parts to a full name:

John   *Fitzgerald*   *Kennedy*
first name (given name)   middle name or initial   last name (family name)

1 WRITE YOUR OWN: Print Your Name

Print your name in English on the lines below:

_____   _____   _____
first name   middle name or initial   last name (family name)

2 WRITE YOUR OWN: Block Letters

Block letters are capital letters. Some forms ask you to print your name
in block letters.

Example: | J | O | H | N | | F. | | K | E | N | N | E | D | Y | | | | | |

Print your name in block letters in these blocks.

| | | | | | | | | | | | | | | | | | | | | | | | | | | | | | | | | |

3 ON THE BOARD: Printing Legibly

Print your name on the board. If the rest of the class can read it, it is
legible. If they cannot read your name, it is illegible. Practice printing.

Writing Upper-Case Letters
(Capital Letters)

1 WRITE YOUR OWN: Tracing Capital Letters
Follow the arrows to trace these written capital letters.

Writing Lower-Case Letters
(Small Letters)

1 WRITE YOUR OWN: Trace the Lower-Case Letters.
Follow the arrows to trace these written lower-case letters.

Size of Upper- And Lower-Case Letters (Handwriting)

1   WITH YOUR CLASS: Height of Lower-Case Letters

Most lower-case cursive letters are one half space high _a_. Some are one whole space high _t_. Some extend one half space below the line _fy_. In writing English, it is important to make the letters the correct height. Whether you write large or small, the relative height of the letters should not change.

height   *height*   *height*

2   WRITE YOUR OWN: Lower-Case Letters

(a)   Practice writing the one half space letters.

a   c   e   i   m   n   o

r   s   u   v   w   x

(b)   Practice writing the whole space letters. Notice that _t_ is not quite a whole space high.

b   d   h   k   l   t

(c)   Practice writing the letters that extend one half space below the line. How is _f_ different from the other letters?

f   g   j   p   q   y   z

3 WITH YOUR CLASS: Different-Sized Letters

Look at the chart below. All upper-case letters fill the space between two lines: *a* . Which upper-case letters also extend below the line?

4 WRITE YOUR OWN: Upper- and Lower-Case Alphabet

Copy the alphabet below. Write each letter the correct size.

Aa Aa Bb Bb Cc Cc
Dd Dd Ee Ee Ff Ff
Gg Gg Hh Hh Ii Ii
Jj Jj Kk Kk Ll Ll
Mm Mm Nn Nn Oo Oo
Pp Pp Qq Qq Rr Rr
Ss Ss Tt Tt Uu Uu
Vv Vv Ww Ww Xx Xx
Yy Yy Zz Zz

Attaching Lower-Case Letters (Handwriting)

1   WITH YOUR CLASS: Attaching Lower-Case Letters That End on the Line

Read this information:

Lower-case letters are attached in handwriting. The final stroke of most letters is on the line: *a* . The letters that follow them must begin on the line: *ab* .

2   WRITE YOUR OWN: Combining Letters That End on the Line

Most letters end like *a* . Their final stroke is on the line. Trace and copy the letters of the alphabet attached to *a* on the line.

3   WRITE YOUR OWN: Combining Other Letters That End on the Line

The other letters that end on the line are *c, d, e, f, g, h, i, j, k, l, m, n, p, q, r, s, t, u, x, y, z*. Practice combining these letters of the alphabet.

12

4 WITH YOUR CLASS: Attaching Letters that End Above the Line

Read this information: The final stroke of b, o, v and w is above the line. Trace and copy the letters of the alphabet attached to b, o, v, w.

[Handwriting practice lines with traced cursive letter combinations]

5 WRITE YOUR OWN: Attaching Letters to b, o, v, w

Practice combining letters with b, v, o, and w.

[Blank handwriting practice lines]

Writing Your Signature

Many forms require your signature. A signature makes a statement or document official; you also use it on checks and business letters.

1 WRITE YOUR OWN: Your Signature

Sign your full name using handwriting. Write your first name or initial. Write your middle name or initial. Write your full last name.

_____

(your signature)

2 WRITE YOUR OWN: Signing a Form

Many times you must sign an affirmation of your statements on a form. Read and sign this affirmation.

I hereby affirm that all these statements are true to the best of my knowledge and belief.

_____

(signature must be full and legible)

3 WITH YOUR CLASS: Forms in This Book

In the Index, find forms where you must write your signature. How many can you find? Write the names of the forms and the page numbers below.

_____   _____

_____   _____

_____   _____

_____   _____

_____   _____

4 ON THE BOARD: Your Signature in Your Native Language

Write your whole name on the board in your native language. Is it the same as your signature in English? Read your name to the class.

Writing Legibly

1   WITH YOUR CLASS: Recognizing Other People's Handwriting
Everyone writes a little bit differently. Can you recognize all these upper-case letters? Look at them with your class.

A B C D D D F F F G H H
L J K K K L L L M M M M
N O P Q Q R R R S S S T
T U U V V V W W W X X
X X Y Z Z Z Z

2   ON THE BOARD: Writing Upper-Case Letters Legibly
Write the upper-case alphabet on the board. Can everyone in the class read all your letters? If they cannot read your writing, practice writing more upper-case letters.

3   WITH YOUR CLASS: Handwriting Style
Handwriting style has changed over the years. In the late 1700's, John Hancock, the first signer of the United States of Americas' Declaration of Independence, signed his name with more precision than John Kennedy did in the 1960's:

John Hancock   *John F. Kennedy*

Time Abbreviations

Numbers are used to write time. You can write "two o'clock in the afternoon" in an abbreviated form—"2:00 p.m." This is the most common way of writing time. A.M. (or a.m.) stands for *ante meridiem* (the first twelve hours of the day). P.M. (or p.m.) stands for *post meridiem* (the last twelve hours of the day).

The chart below shows more examples of time abbreviations:

7:00 a.m.	seven o'clock in the morning
12:00 p.m.	twelve o'clock noon
3:15 p.m.	three-fifteen in the afternoon
6:30 p.m.	six-thirty in the evening
11:45 a.m.	eleven forty-five in the morning
12:00 a.m.	twelve o'clock midnight

1 WRITE YOUR OWN: Writing Time Abbreviations

Using the chart, change these words to number abbreviations. Check your answers with your class.

1. two forty-five in the afternoon _____
2. noon _____
3. ten-twenty at night _____
4. seven-thirty in the evening _____
5. four-fifteen in the afternoon _____
6. midnight _____
7. five o'clock in the morning _____

2 WITH YOUR PARTNER: Answering Questions Using Time Abbreviations

Answer these questions using time abbreviations. Then read your answers to your partner.

1. What time do you get up on Sunday? _____
2. What time do you get up on weekdays? _____
3. What time can you watch the news on TV? _____
4. What time does this class end? _____
5. What time does the New Year begin? _____

Writing Dates

1 WRITE YOUR OWN: Months
Copy the months (print or use handwriting)

January	_____	July	_____
February	_____	August	_____
March	_____	September	_____
April	_____	October	_____
May	_____	November	_____
June	_____	December	_____

2 WRITE YOUR OWN: Dates
Write dates in English these three ways:

January 22, 1983

Jan. 22, 1983

1/22/83

Copy these dates:

1. February 14, 1960 _____

Feb. 14, 1960 _____

2/14/60 _____

2. March 2, 1938 _____

Mar. 2, 1938 _____

3/22/38 _____

3. October 22, 1974 _____

Oct. 22, 1974 _____

10/22/74 _____

4. July 6, 1972* _____

7/6/72 _____

5. June 22, 1944* _____

6/22/44 _____

* May, June, and July are rarely abbreviated.

6. November 19, 1969 _____
   Nov. 19, 1969 _____
   11/19/69 _____

7. September 23, 1916 _____
   Sept. 23, 1916 _____
   9/23/16 _____

8. January 9, 1952 _____
   Jan. 9, 1952 _____
   1/9/52 _____

9. April 1, 1923 _____
   Apr. 1, 1923 _____
   4/1/23 _____

10. May 13, 1921 _____
    5/13/21 _____

11. August 4, 1903 _____
    Aug. 4, 1903 _____
    8/4/03 _____

12. Today's date: _____

_____ _____

_____ _____

_____ _____

3 ON THE BOARD: Dates in Other Countries
Write today's date in your native language on the board. How is it different from American dates?

4 WRITE YOUR OWN: Birthdates
Write your birthdate in three ways:

_____

_____

_____

5 WITH A PARTNER: Your Classmates' Birthdates
Write your partner's birthdate three ways:

_____

_____

_____

6 WITH YOUR CLASS: Writing Date of Birth (D.O.B.) on Forms

Some forms ask for your birthdate. (See Health Insurance Application, page 110, and Driver's License Application, page 116.) Study the various types of forms below and fill in your birthdate.

1.

Month	Day	Year

2.

Mo	Da	Yr

3. _____

4. _____ / _____ / _____

5. Month: _____ Date: _____ Year: _____

6. [　　　]   [　　　]   [　　　]

19

CHAPTER FOLLOW-UP

1 Look in the Index under **Handwriting** to find the writing tasks in this book that are usually handwritten.

2 Look in the Index under **Printing** to find the writing tasks in this book that are usually printed.

3 Look in the Index under **Numbers** to find the writing tasks in this book that involve numbers.

4 Why is it useful to write legibly? Have you ever had a problem because of illegible handwriting?

5 Where do you need to write dates?

6 Some historical dates in the United States are:

> April 19, 1775 (Paul Revere's ride—Battles of Concord and Lexington—the start of the American Revolution)
> July 4, 1776 (Declaration of Independence)
> November 11, 1918 (Armistice Day, end of World War I)
> July 21, 1969 (Man walked on the moon for the first time)

Discuss these events with your teacher.

7 What are some historical dates in your native country? Write them on the board and explain them to the class.

8 If you are unfamiliar with writing using the Roman alphabet, do extra practice in tracing and writing at home. With patience and regular practice, you will be able to write legibly and easily in English.

Personal Writing

Teacher's Notes

Student Objectives:
- to practice writing in English
- to become comfortable writing about your life and expressing your opinions in English.

Sequence

1 Tell the students not to write anything until the class has discussed the page.

2 To preview the chapter, explain what a journal is. Ask students if they have ever kept a journal in their native language. Ask them what they wrote about in their journals.

3 Discuss these potential benefits for ESL students of keeping a daily journal in English:

    a To become comfortable expressing their thoughts and feelings in English

    b To keep a record of their experiences for the future

    c To reinforce their English writing skills by writing every day in English

    d To practice writing, in context, vocabulary that is relevant to their personal lives.

4 The other two pages in this chapter introduce students to two other personal writing tasks, writing a personal schedule and writing a personal opinion telegram.

    a Preview the personal schedule page by asking the students if they ever write schedules of their activities. Discuss different ways of writing down scheduled activities—for example, an appointment book, a calendar, a list of things to do.

    b Preview the personal opinion telegram page by asking the students these questions:

        1 Is it customary to send personal opinion telegrams to government officials in your native country?

        2 If not, are people in your native country permitted to express political opinions openly, and how do they customarily express them?

5 Provide a model of each journal entry and the personal opinion telegram by reading it aloud, using the vocabulary from the list.

6 Discuss the vocabulary on each page. Write the students' suggestions for *other* vocabulary on the board. Have the students copy these words in their books.

7 Have the students fill in the model on each page and complete the other exercises on the page.

Daily Journal—Personal Information

A journal is a record of your thoughts and experiences. Writing a daily journal in English will help you to improve your handwriting and vocabulary.

1 WITH YOUR CLASS: Vocabulary

Read the journal entry below with your class and add more words to the vocabulary list.

2 WRITE YOUR OWN: Journal Entry

Fill in the journal entry with personal information.

~JOURNAL~

_____
(1)

Today I am going to write about myself. I come from _____ and I speak _____.
(2)
(3)
I was born on _____.
(4)
I am _____ years old.
(5)
I am _____ and
(6)
I have _____.
(7)
I live _____
(8)
in _____.
(9)

1. *Today's date*
2. *Your native country*
3. *The languages you speak*
4. *Your birthdate*
5. *Your age*
6. *Choose one:*
    • married
    • single
    • divorced
    • separated
    • widowed
7. *Choose one:*
    • no children
    • one child
    • two children
    • *other:* _____
    _____
    _____
8. *Choose one:*
    • by myself
    • with my family
    • with a friend
    • with relatives
    • with friends
    • *other:* _____
    _____
    _____
9. *Name of the town and state you live in*

3 WITH YOUR PARTNER: Reading Entries

Read your journal entry to your partner. Listen to your partner's journal entry; then tell the class about your partner.

Daily Journal—Weather

1 WITH YOUR CLASS: Vocabulary
Read this journal entry. Add more words to the vocabulary list below.

2 WRITE YOUR OWN: Journal Entry
Fill in the journal entry to tell about the weather today.

JOURNAL

_____
(1)

Today is a _____
(2)

day. It is very _____.
(3)

It is a good day to

_____ .
(4)

1. *Today's date*
2. *Choose one:*
   - rainy
   - cloudy
   - sunny
   - windy
   - snowy
   - *other:* _____

   _____

3. *Choose one:*
   - hot
   - mild
   - cold
   - cool
   - warm
   - *other:* _____

   _____

4. *Choose one:*
   - shovel snow
   - go to the beach
   - go to the movies
   - study English
   - sleep
   - *other:* _____

   _____

   _____

3 WRITE YOUR OWN: Journal Practice
Every day for one week write a journal entry about the weather for that day.

Daily Journal—In the Morning

1 WITH YOUR CLASS: Vocabulary

Read the journal entry and add more words to the vocabulary list below.

2 WRITE YOUR OWN: Journal Entry

Fill in the journal entry to tell about your morning today.

JOURNAL

_____ (1)

Today I got up at _____ (2) .

I _____ (3)

and _____ (3) .

I had _____ (4)

for breakfast. This morning

I felt _____ (5) .

1. *Today's date*
2. *The time you got up*
3. *Choose one:*
    • got dressed
    • washed my face
    • took a shower
    • shaved
    • brushed my teeth
    • combed my hair
    • *other:* _____

    _____

4. *Choose one or more:*
    • nothing
    • a cup of coffee
    • an egg
    • a piece of toast
    • *other:* _____

    _____

5. *Choose one:*
    • energetic
    • sleepy
    • wonderful
    • terrible
    • cheerful
    • grouchy
    • *other:* _____

    _____

    _____

3 WRITE YOUR OWN: Journal Practice

Every day for one week write a journal entry about your morning that day.

Personal Schedule

1 WITH YOUR PARTNER: List of Things to Do

Write a list of things you plan to do tomorrow. Compare your list with your partner's list. Is anything the same on both lists? Who has more interesting things to do tomorrow? Tell the class about your partner's plans.

2 WRITE YOUR OWN: Daily Activities Schedule

When you are very busy, a schedule helps to organize your time. Fill in this schedule with your activities for today.

DAILY ACTIVITIES SCHEDULE	
Day: _____	Date: _____
6:00 a.m. _____	4:00 p.m. _____
7:00 a.m. _____	5:00 p.m. _____
8:00 a.m. _____	6:00 p.m. _____
9:00 a.m. _____	7:00 p.m. _____
10:00 a.m. _____	8:00 p.m. _____
11:00 a.m. _____	9:00 p.m. _____
12:00 p.m. _____	10:00 p.m. _____
1:00 p.m. _____	11:00 p.m. _____
2:00 p.m. _____	12:00 a.m. _____
3:00 p.m. _____	1:00 a.m. _____

3 WRITE YOUR OWN: Schedules

Writing schedules in English is good practice for vocabulary and handwriting. Write a schedule of your activities every day for a week.

Daily Journal—Today

1 WITH YOUR CLASS: Vocabulary

Read the journal entry. Add more words to the vocabulary list below.

2 WRITE YOUR OWN: Journal Entry

Fill in the journal entry to tell about your day.

JOURNAL

_____
(1)

Today I am feeling

_____ . I
(2)

have been _____
(3)

all day. Now I am

going to _____ .
(4)

1. *Today's date*
2. *Choose one:*
   • happy
   • fine
   • homesick
   • nervous
   • bored
   • frustrated
   • depressed
   • *other:* _____
   _____
   _____

3. *Choose one:*
   • working
   • studying
   • shopping
   • cooking
   • cleaning
   • doing nothing
   • doing many things
   • *other:* _____
   _____
   _____

4. *Choose one:*
   • eat
   • sleep
   • study
   • watch TV
   • go out
   • *other:* _____
   _____
   _____

3 WRITE YOUR OWN: Journal Practice

Every day for one week write a journal entry about your feelings and activities for that day.

Daily Journal—Thinking About Life

1 WITH YOUR CLASS: Vocabulary
Read the journal entry and add more words to the vocabulary list below.

2 WITH YOUR PARTNER: Thinking About Yourself
Fill in the journal entry to tell about yourself. Then compare yourself with your partner. Did you write any of the same things? Tell the class about your partner.

JOURNAL

_____
(1)

I have been thinking about myself today. I think I am basically a _____ person.
(2)

I enjoy _____
(3)
very much, and I love

_____.

One thing I don't like
(4)
to do is_____.
(5)

1. *Today's date*
2. *Choose one:*
   - practical
   - creative
   - fun-loving
   - quiet
   - *other:* _____

   _____

3. *Choose one:*
   - being alone
   - being with people
   - studying
   - working
   - *other:* _____

   _____

4. *Choose one:*
   - to travel
   - to play ping pong
   - to watch TV
   - to go out with my friends
   - *other:* _____

   _____

5. *Choose one:*
   - fight
   - be alone
   - go to parties
   - get drunk
   - be bored
   - *other:* _____

   _____

Daily Journal—Beliefs and Opinions

1 WITH YOUR CLASS: Vocabulary
Read the journal entry. Add more words to the vocabulary list below.

2 WITH YOUR PARTNER: Personal Opinion Entry
Fill in this journal entry. Then compare it with your partner's entry. Share your opinion with your partner.

JOURNAL

_____
(1)

I have strong opinions about_____ .
(2)

I _____ talk about
(3)

my beliefs, because most of the people around me

_____
(4)

1. *Today's date*
2. *Choose one:*
   • politics
   • religion
   • marriage
   • family life
   • *other:* _____
   _____

3. *Choose one:*
   • often
   • rarely
   • *other:* _____
   _____
   _____

4. *Choose one:*
   • agree with me
   • don't agree with me
   • are interested
   • aren't interested
   • are strangers
   • are my friends

3 WRITE YOUR OWN: Opinions and Beliefs
Write one or more journal entries in your own words about what you think and believe.

Personal Opinion Telegram

You can send a personal opinion telegram to an elected official. A personal opinion telegram tells how you feel about a problem or policy and makes suggestions. It costs about half the price of a regular telegram.

1 WITH YOUR CLASS: Telegram to the President of the United States

Complete this personal opinion telegram.

MSG. NO.	NO. WDS CL. OF SVC.	PD.—COLL.	CASH NO.	ACCOUNTING INFORMATION	DATE	FILING TIME	SENT TIME

western union   **Telegram**

A.M. P.M.   A.M. P.M.

SEND THE FOLLOWING MESSAGE, SUBJECT TO THE TERMS ON BACK HEREOF, WHICH ARE HEREBY AGREED TO.

☐ OVERNIGHT TELEGRAM
UNLESS BOX ABOVE IS CHECKED THIS MESSAGE WILL BE SENT AS A TELEGRAM.

(1) TO _____ CARE OF OR APARTMENT NO.

(2) ADDRESS & TELEPHONE NO. _____

CITY — STATE & ZIP CODE

(3) _____

(4) _____

(5) _____

(6) _____

(7, 8) SENDER'S TEL. NO.   NAME & ADDRESS

OFFICE USE ONLY

EOM

(BILL TO)   (ADDRESS)   (CITY - STATE - ZIP)   (CHG. METH.)

X-OFF

(CHG.#)   (OPR.#)   (HF)   (PC CODE)   (PC AMT.)   (GIFT AMT.)   (TAX)   (AGT. I.D.)   (SG)

Telegram form courtesy of Western Union Telegraph Co.

1. *Name of the President*

2. The White House, Washington, D.C.

3. *Choose one:*
   - I like
   - I don't like

4. *Choose one*
   - what you are doing about
   - what you did about
   - what you said about

5. *Choose a controversial issue*

6. *Choose one:*
   - Please reconsider.
   - Thank you.
   - Keep up the good work.
   - We're behind you.
   - I won't vote for you again.

7. *Your telephone number*

8. *Your name and address*

2 ON THE BOARD: Personal Opinion Telegram
With your class, write a personal opinion telegram to your U.S. Senator, your Governor, your State Senator, your U.S. Representative or your State Representative.

CHAPTER FOLLOW-UP

1 Write a journal entry about a friend or relative you know well. Use the vocabulary from page 28 or add more.

2 Think about these questions: What do you want to accomplish in your life? Write a journal entry in your own words to answer these questions.

3 Make a list on the board of possible journal topics. Choose the topics that interest you and write about them in your journal. Continue writing a daily journal throughout this course.

4 Write a list of things you have to do today. What is the difference between a *Things To Do* list and a *Daily Schedule?*

5 As a class project, at the beginning of every month, make a calendar for that month on poster board. Fill in the calendar with the following information:

   a   Birthdays of students in the class
   b   United States holidays occurring in that month
   c   Your native country's national holidays occurring that month
   d   Class activities for that month
   e   School events for that month

6 Look up **Telegrams** in the Index. What other telegrams are included in this book?

7 Make a list on the board of the names of these government officials (see **Addressing Envelopes: Abbreviations and Titles** in Chapter 3 for abbreviations of official titles).

   a   President of the United States
   b   Vice President of the United States
   c   U.S. Senators for your state (two)
   d   U.S. Representative from your congressional district
   e   Governor of your state
   f   Your State Senator
   g   Your State Representative
   h   A local government official

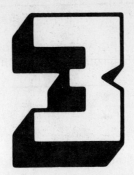

Addresses and Postal Services

Teacher's Notes

Student Objectives:
- to learn to address an envelope
- to learn to fill out forms from the post office.

Sequence

1 Tell the students not to write anything until the class has discussed the page.

2 Preview the first eight pages by looking at the sample envelope first and studying the vocabulary. Preview the other pages by discussing the vocabulary on each of the printed forms. Write the words on the board.

3 On each page, have the students compare the way each part of the address and its special instructions are written in the United States with the way this is done in their native countries. Do other countries use zip codes? abbreviations? ordinal numbers in street names? other special instructions? Point out that periods are not always used after some abbreviations.

4 Have the students complete the exercises or fill in the forms.

5 Check answers when appropriate.

Sample Envelope

1   WITH YOUR CLASS: Vocabulary
Look at this sample envelope and find these parts:

1.   Name of sender
2.   Address of sender
3.   Title of addressee
4.   Name of addressee
5.   Street address
6.   Apartment number
7.   City
8.   State
9.   Zip code
10. Stamp
11. Postmark

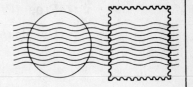

P.J. Gomez
32 Lakeview Rd.
Hilldale, MA 01824

Dr. William Rutledge
1508 S. Summit Ave. Apt. 6E
Hilldale, Massachusetts 01824

Addressing Envelopes: Abbreviations of Titles

An *abbreviation* is a short way to write a word. Use a period after an abbreviation.

1   WITH YOUR CLASS: Abbreviations of Titles
Copy these abbreviations of titles we use before people's names.

Ms. (pronounced *miz*, but never written out)   _____

Mrs. (pronounced *missus,* but never written out)   _____

Mr. (Mister—the abbreviation is almost always used)   _____

Miss (This title is never abbreviated)   _____

Dr. (Doctor)   _____

Prof. (Professor)   _____

Gov. (Governor)   _____

Sen. (Senator)   _____

Rep. (Representative)   _____

Pres. (President)   _____

Dir. (Director)   _____

2   WRITE YOUR OWN: Choosing a Title
Write the abbreviation for the following people:

1.   a man   _____

2.   a married woman   _____

3.   a single woman   _____

4.   a girl   _____

5.   a dentist   _____

6.   the President   _____

7.   your title   _____

3   ON THE BOARD: Other Titles
There are many other titles that we use before people's names. On the board, write other titles you know. Use a dictionary to help you.

Addressing Envelopes:
Abbreviations of Street Addresses

1 WRITE YOUR OWN: Abbreviations

Write out the entire word first; then write the abbreviation for these street addresses.

Word	Abbreviation	Copy the Word	Copy the Abbreviation
Street	St.	_____	_____
Road	Rd.	_____	_____
Avenue	Ave.	_____	_____
Court	Ct.	_____	_____
Square	Sq.	_____	_____
Lane	La.	_____	_____
Park	Pk.	_____	_____
Boulevard	Blvd.	_____	_____
Drive	Dr.	_____	_____
North	N.	_____	_____
South	S.	_____	_____
East	E.	_____	_____
West	W.	_____	_____
Northeast	N.E.	_____	_____
Northwest	N.W.	_____	_____
Southeast	S.E.	_____	_____
Southwest	S.W.	_____	_____
Apartment	Apt.	_____	_____
Rural Free Delivery	R.F.D.	_____	_____
Post Office Box	P.O. Box	_____	_____

2 WRITE YOUR OWN: Street Address

Write your street address without abbreviations.

_____

Write your street address with abbreviations.

_____

Streets With Ordinal Numbers

Ordinal numbers show order or position in a series of numbers. The names of some streets are ordinal numbers. (Example: Fifth Avenue in New York City.)

1 WITH YOUR CLASS: Spelling Ordinal Numbers

Look at the ordinal numbers on this chart. Notice that you add *th* to most of the numerals. The exceptions are *first* (1st) *second* (2nd), and *third* (3rd) wherever they occur. The spelling of some of the other ordinal numbers is irregular: *fifth, eighth, ninth,* and *twelfth.* For all numbers which end with *y*, change the *y* to *i* and add *-eth*.

ORDINAL NUMBERS

1st	first	21st	twenty-first
2nd	second	22nd	twenty-second
3rd	third	23rd	twenty-third
4th	fourth	24th	twenty-fourth
5th	fifth	25th	twenty-fifth
6th	sixth	26th	twenty-sixth
7th	seventh	27th	twenty-seventh
8th	eighth	28th	twenty-eighth
9th	ninth	29th	twenty-ninth
10th	tenth	30th	thirtieth
11th	eleventh	40th	fortieth
12th	twelfth	50th	fiftieth
13th	thirteenth	60th	sixtieth
14th	fourteenth	70th	seventieth
15th	fifteenth	80th	eightieth
16th	sixteenth	90th	ninetieth
17th	seventeenth	100th	one hundredth
18th	eighteenth	200th	two hundredth
19th	nineteenth		
20th	twentieth		

2 WRITE YOUR OWN: List of Ordinal Numbers

Copy these ordinal numbers in your notebook. Spell them carefully.

3 WRITE YOUR OWN: Streets with Ordinal Numbers

Change the number words to numerals and abbreviate *Street* or *Avenue*.

1. Twenty-first Street _____
2. Eighth Avenue _____
3. Fifty-second Street _____
4. Second Avenue _____
5. Seventy-third Street _____

4 WRITE YOUR OWN: Streets with Ordinal Numbers

Change the numerals to number words. Write out the words *St.* and *Ave.*

1. 12th Ave. _____
2. 9th Ave. _____
3. 58th St. _____
4. 45th St. _____
5. 60th St. _____

5 WITH A PARTNER: Local Streets with Ordinal Numbers

Do the streets where you live have ordinal numbers? Look at the street signs. Are the numbers written in words or numerals? With your partner, prepare a list of local streets with ordinal numbers. Share your list with the class.

Addressing Envelopes: States, Zip Codes, and Countries

1 WITH YOUR CLASS: State Abbreviations

Review this list of state names and abbreviations. Write the correct abbreviations on the map on the next page.

Alabama
    (Ala. or AL)
Alaska (AK)
Arizona
    (Ariz. or AZ)
Arkansas
    (Ark. or AR)
California
    (Calif. or CA)
Colorado
    (Colo. or CO)
Connecticut
    (Conn. or CT)
Delaware
    (Del. or DE)
District of Columbia
    (D.C. or DC)
Florida (Fla. or FL)
Georgia (Ga. or GA)
Hawaii (HI)
Idaho (ID)
Illinois (Ill. or IL)
Indiana (Ind. or IN)
Iowa (IA)
Kansas (Kans. or KS)
Kentucky (Ky. or KY)
Louisiana
    (La. or LA)

Maine (Me. or ME)
Maryland (Md. or MD)
Massachusetts
    (Mass. or MA)
Michigan
    (Mich. or MI)
Minnesota
    (Minn. or MN)
Mississippi
    (Miss. or MS)
Missouri
    (Mo. or MO)
Montana
    (Mont. or MT)
Nebraska
    (Nebr. or NB)
Nevada (Nev. or NV)
New Hampshire
    (N.H. or NH)
New Jersey
    (N.J. or NJ)
New Mexico
    (N. Mex. or NM)
New York
    (N.Y. or NY)
North Carolina
    (N.C. or NC)
North Dakota
    (N.Dak. or ND)

Ohio (OH)
Oklahoma
    (Okla. or OK)
Oregon
    (Oreg. or OR)
Pennsylvania
    (Penna., Pa., or PA)
Rhode Island
    (R.I. or RI)
South Carolina
    (S.C. or SC)
South Dakota
    (S. Dak. or SD)
Tennessee
    (Tenn. or TN)
Texas (Tex. or TX)
Utah (UT)
Vermont (Vt. or VT)
Virginia (Va. or VA)
Washington
    (Wash. or WA)
West Virginia
    (W.Va. or WV)
Wisconsin
    (Wis. or WI)
Wyoming
    (Wyo. or WY)

2 **WRITE YOUR OWN:** Zip Codes

Your *zip code* is the group of numbers added at the end of your address. This *Zone Improvement Program* was started by the U.S. Postal Service in 1963. It helps the Post Office to sort the mail more efficiently.

Write your state and zip code below. Use the state abbreviation.

_____

3 **ON THE BOARD:** Abbreviations of Names of Countries

Make a list of all countries you can think of that have names which can be abbreviated. Copy the list in your notebook. (Example: United Kingdom—U.K.)

Addresses

Notice the order of information in an address in the United States.

350	North Avenue
(number)	(street name)

Danvers,	Massachusetts	01923
(city)	(state)	(zip code)

1 WRITE YOUR OWN: Writing Your Address in the United States

a. Write your street address _____

b. Write your city or town _____

c. Write your state and zip code _____

2 WITH A PARTNER: Writing Other Addresses in the United States

a. Write your partner's name _____

b. Write your partner's street address _____

c. Write your partner's city or town _____

d. Write your partner's state and zip code _____

3 ON THE BOARD: Writing Addresses in Other Countries

Write the address of a relative in your native country. Write the address in your native language and in English. Compare the way addresses are written in different countries.

Addressing An Envelope

When you mail a letter, include an address and a return address on the envelope. If the letter cannot be delivered, the post office will return it to you.

1 WITH A PARTNER: Addressing an Envelope

Fill in the return address and the address on this sample envelope.

Return Address	*Address*
1. *Your name*	5. *Your partner's name*
2. *Your street address*	6. *Your partner's street address*
3. *Your city or town*	7. *Your partner's city or town*
4. *Your state and zip code*	8. *Your partner's state and zip code*

_____ (1)

_____ (2)

_____ (3)

_____ (4)

_____ (5)

_____ (6)

_____ (7)

_____ (8)

Envelopes With Special Instructions

1   WRITE YOUR OWN: Special Instructions (Air Mail—
   Photo Enclosed—Please Forward)

Address this envelope to a friend or relative. If you are sending the letter
by air mail, write **Air Mail** on the envelope. If you are sending a
photograph, write **Photo Enclosed.** If your friend or relative has moved
and you don't know the new address, write **Please Forward.** Write your
return address.

Write
special
instructions
here ——————➤

2 WRITE YOUR OWN: In Care Of (c/o)

c/o means "in care of." Use c/o if the person who is to receive the letter is living with a family that has a different name.

Hai Nguyen is living with the Nassar family in Chicago, Illinois. Copy his address on the envelope below. Write your own return address.

Mr. Hai Nguyen
c/o Nassar
1194 W. Foster Avenue
Chicago, Illinois 60625

45

Post Office—Change of Address

When you move to a new address, fill out a *Change of Address* card at your old post office. Then the post office will *forward your mail.* (The post office will send your mail to your new address.) Who else should you send your new address to?

1 WITH YOUR CLASS: Change of Address Order

Fill out both sides of this sample card. Be sure to write your former address and your current address.

☆ U.S. GPO: 1978—753-331

THIS ORDER PROVIDES for the forwarding of first-class mail and all parcels of obvious value for a period not to exceed 1 year.	Print or Type *(Last Name, First Name, Middle Initial)*

CHANGE OF ADDRESS IS FOR:

☐ Entire Family *(When last name of family members differ, separate orders for each last name must be filed)*

☐ Individual Signer Only

I AGREE TO PAY FORWARDING POSTAGE FOR MAGAZINES FOR 90 DAYS

☐ NO ☐ YES

OLD ADDRESS

No. and St., Apt., Suite, P.O. Box or R.D. No. (In care of)

Post Office, State and ZIP Code

NEW ADDRESS

No. and St., Apt., Suite, P.O. Box or R.D. No. (In care of)

Post Office, State and ZIP Code

USPS USE ONLY

CLERK/ CARRIER ENDORSEMENT

CARRIER ROUTE NUMBER

Effective Date | If Temporary, Expiration Date

DATE ENTERED

Sign Here ▶ | Date Signed

PS Form 3575, May 1978

Signature & title of person authorizing address change. (DO NOT print or type)

CHANGE OF ADDRESS ORDER

MAIL OR DELIVER TO POST OFFICE OF <u>OLD</u> ADDRESS

AFFIX FIRST-CLASS POSTAGE IF MAILED

To ____ **POSTMASTER** ____

City ____

State ____ ZIP ____

46

Parcel Post Customs Declaration

When you mail a package from the United States to another country, you must fill out a *Parcel Post Customs Declaration.*

1 WITH A PARTNER: Customs Declaration List

Below is a list of possible items to send to a friend or relative in another country. Add other items you would send and write their value.

Item	Value
5 children's toys	40.00
1 man's shirt	11.00
2 bedsheets	20.00
1 typewriter	210.00
1 wristwatch	85.00

Other: _____   _____

_____   _____

_____   _____

2 WITH YOUR CLASS: Filling out the Parcel Post Customs Declaration Label

Choose three items from your list. Write them under *Itemized List of Contents.* Write the quantity (*Qty*) and the value (*U.S. dollars*) of each item. Complete the *Instructions Given By Sender.* Sign on the *Sender's Signature* line.

THIS LABEL FOR INTERNATIONAL PARCEL POST USE. COMPLETE AND APPLY ON ADDRESS SIDE OF PARCEL. BEND AT SLIT AND PEEL OFF BACKING.

PARCEL POST CUSTOMS DECLARATION — UNITED STATES OF AMERICA

INSTRUCTIONS GIVEN BY SENDER *Dispositions de l'Expéditeur*	QTY	USE INK OR TYPEWRITER ITEMIZED LIST OF CONTENTS	VALUE (U.S. $)

If undeliverable as addressed:
Au cas de non-livraison:

☐ Return to sender. Return charges guaranteed.
Le colis doit être renvoyé à l'expéditeur, qui s'engage à payer les frais de retour.

☐ Forward to. (*Le colis doit être réexpédié à*):

☐ Abandon. (*Abandon du colis.*)

(Sender's Signature—*Signature de l'expéditeur*)

MAILING OFFICE DATE STAMP

LBS.

OZS.

POSTAGE $

ACCEPTING CLERK'S INITIALS

INSURED VALUE (U.S. $)

PS Form 2966-A, June 1972

47

Complaint At The Post Office

If you have a complaint or a suggestion for the post office, fill out a *Consumer Service Card.*

1 WITH YOUR CLASS: Consumer Service Card
Read this card together. Then fill it in for the following situation. (Look up the address of the Immigration and Naturalization Service in your area.)

Situation: A certified letter you received from the Immigration and Naturalization Service arrived opened with the documents missing.

---

(1) COMPLETE BELOW. PRINT FIRMLY.   **(2) REMOVE THIS TAB.** DISCARD CARBON.   **(3) FILL IN ADDRESS BLANK** ON CARD TO YOUR POSTMASTER.   **(4) MAIL** BOTH CARDS.

☆ U.S. GOVERNMENT PRINTING OFFICE: 1975-588-822

CONSUMER SERVICE CARD

Date: _____
mo.   day   year

A1627843

Name	Address	City	State	ZIP	Day Phone

● Is this: Information request ☐   Suggestion ☐   Complaint ☐   Other ☐

● If this is a problem with a specific mailing, please complete following:

Please give information on the other person involved in this mailing:

Was it:
☐ Letter
☐ Regular Parcel Post
☐ Air Parcel Post
☐ Newspaper/ Magazine
☐ Advertisement

Was mailing:
☐ 1st Class
☐ Airmail
☐ Special Delivery
☐ Certified
☐ Registered
☐ Insured

Did it involve:
☐ Delay
☐ Non-receipt
☐ Damage

Name _____
Address _____
City _____
State _____ ZIP _____

Was the above person   ☐ Sender   ☐ Receiver

● If not specific mail problem, is it: ☐ Self Service Postal Equipment   ☐ Money Order   ☐ Postal personnel

● Please give essential facts: _____
_____
_____
_____

PS Form 4314-July 1975   Thank you. You will be contacted soon.

Alien Address Report

Every year in January all aliens living or working in the United States must fill out an *Alien Address Report.* An *alien* is a person who is not a citizen of the United States: an immigrant, a visitor, a student, a crewman, a diplomat, or a refugee. You can get an Alien Address Report from the post office or the Immigration and Naturalization Service Office. Mail the card to:

U.S. Immigration and Naturalization
Arlington, Virginia 22218

1 WITH YOUR CLASS: Alien Address Report

Read this form and discuss the vocabulary with your class.

2 WRITE YOUR OWN: Alien Address Report Form

Practice filling out this sample Alien Address Report.

ALIEN ADDRESS REPORT COMPLETE ALL ITEMS—PRINT IN BLOCK LETTERS WITH BALL-POINT PEN OR USE TYPEWRITER. THIS CARD MUST BE MAILED. PLACE A TEN CENT U.S. POSTAGE STAMP ON REVERSE AND DROP IN MAIL BOX. THIS CARD IS REVISED ANNUALLY. ONLY SUBMIT A CURRENT YEAR CARD.

1. (LAST NAME)   (FIRST)   (MIDDLE)

2. ADDRESS IN THE U.S. (EXCEPT COMMUTERS—SHOW ADDRESS IN MEXICO OR CANADA. SEE ITEM 15)

CITY OR TOWN	STATE	ZIP CODE	CHECK HERE IF ADDRESS IS CURRENT ☐

3. ALIEN NO. FROM ALIEN CARD A-

4. PLACE ENTERED THE U.S.

5. WHEN ENTERED U.S. (MO/DAY/YR)

6. SEX ☐ MALE ☐ FEMALE

7. COUNTRY OF BIRTH

8. DATE OF BIRTH (MO/DAY/YR)

9. COUNTRY OF CITIZENSHIP

10. ARE YOU NOW WORKING IN THE U.S.? ☐ YES ☐ NO

11. SOCIAL SECURITY NO. (IF ANY)

12. FOR GOVERNMENT USE ONLY

13. PRESENT OR MOST RECENT OCCUPATION IN U.S. (MAIN JOB)

14. TYPE OF FIRM OR BUSINESS OF PRESENT OR MOST RECENT EMPLOYMENT (MAIN JOB)

15. STATUS (CHECK APPROPRIATE BOX) WHEN DID YOU RECEIVE YOUR PRESENT IMMIGRATION STATUS? (MO/DAY/YR)_____

1 ☐ IMMIGRANT (PERMANENT RESIDENT)   3 ☐ VISITOR   4 ☐ CREWMAN   5 ☐ STUDENT

2 ☐ IMMIGRANT (COMMUTER WORKER-CHECK THIS BLOCK   6 ☐ EXCHANGE ALIEN   7 ☐ REFUGEE-PAROLEE

IF YOU ENTER THE U.S. DAILY OR AT LEAST TWICE A WEEK)   8 ☐ OTHER (SPECIFY)_____

16. I CERTIFY THAT THE STATEMENTS ON THIS CARD ARE TRUE TO THE BEST OF MY KNOWLEDGE

SIGNATURE (IF UNDER 14 YEARS OLD, SIGNATURE OF PARENT OR GUARDIAN)   DATE

Form I-53 (Rev.1-1-80)N   U.S. DEPARTMENT OF JUSTICE—IMMIGRATION AND NATURALIZATION SERVICE FORM APPROVED OMB NO. 43--R0306

CHAPTER FOLLOW-UP

1 Which abbreviations can be used in writing an address?

2 What is an ordinal number? What are some examples?

3 Where else would you use ordinal numbers? Look at **Wedding Anniversary Announcements** for an example.

4 What does the post office do when it *forwards your mail?* On which pages or forms in this chapter is the word *forward* used?

5 What are the services of the U.S. Post Office? List them on the board.

6 Who must fill out an *Alien Address Report?* What are some other forms you can fill out at the post office?

7 Skim this chapter and circle all new vocabulary words. Make a list on the board of the vocabulary you remember from this chapter.

Greetings

Teacher's Notes

Student Objectives:
- *to become familiar with the occasions for which greeting cards are popular in the United States.*
- *to learn to recognize appropriate cards for special occasions.*
- *to practice writing personal messages and greetings.*

Sequence

1 Tell the students not to write anything until each page has been discussed.

2 Provide a model of each card or telegram by reading it aloud, using vocabulary from the list.

3 Discuss the use of greeting cards. When would you send a telegram instead of a card?

4 Share this historical information with the students:

The first written holiday messages were exchanged for Valentine's Day in 1684. It wasn't until the 1840's that Christmas and Valentine's Day cards were commercially produced in London, England. Greeting cards were first printed in the United States in Boston during this period. However, they were all exported to England until 1875, when they were first marketed in the United States. Since then, the greeting card industry has become a multimillion-dollar business in the United States.

5 Have the students complete the cards and telegram in their books.

6 Ask the students to copy the greetings and messages in their notebooks.

7 Complete the other exercises on each page.

Birthday Cards

When you send a birthday card, you sign your name on the card. You may add a personal greeting.

1   WRITE YOUR OWN: Sign a Birthday Card

Fill in the blanks. Then sign the card.

1. *Choose one:*
   - Wishing you a wonderful birthday
   - Hope your birthday is a happy one
   - Best wishes today and always
   - . . . and many, many more
2. *Choose one:*
   - Sincerely
   - Love
   - Fondly
3. *Your signature*

(1)

(2))

(3)

2   WITH YOUR CLASS: Other Birthday Cards

What kind of birthday cards do you like to send? Humorous? Sentimental? List the categories of birthday cards on the board. Bring in a card which you would like to send. Compare it with the other students' cards. Which category does your card illustrate?

3   WITH YOUR CLASS: Happy Birthday in Other Languages

How do you write "Happy Birthday" in your language? Write it on the board. Teach the class the pronunciation.

Mother's Day Cards

The third Sunday in May is Mother's Day. People send cards to mothers to celebrate the occasion.

1   WRITE YOUR OWN: Mother's Day Card
Fill in the blanks. Sign the card.

1. *Date this year*
2. *Choose one:*
   • To the best mother in the world
   • Thinking of you on Mother's Day
   • Thanks, Mom!
3. *Choose one:*
   • With love
   • Love
   • Your loving son
   • Your loving daughter
   • Your grandson
   • Your granddaughter
   • Love always
4. *Sign your first name*

2   ON THE BOARD: Father's Day Card
The third Sunday in June is Father's Day. Write a message for Father's Day on the board.

3   WITH YOUR CLASS: Mother's Day and Father's Day in Your Country
Do people celebrate these holidays in your native country? What is the greeting? Write it on the board.

Get Well Cards

When friends or relatives are sick or injured, get well cards are a good way to cheer them up.

1   WRITE YOUR OWN: Get Well Card
Copy an appropriate message onto the card.

1. *Choose one:*
   • Hope you have a speedy recovery.
   • We are praying for your recovery.
   • Hope you are feeling better.
   • Hope you will be on your feet again soon.
   • We miss you and hope you will be back soon.
2. *Your signature*

2   WITH YOUR CLASS: Humorous Get Well Cards
Bring humorous get well cards to class. Discuss with your class when you could send humorous cards.

3   WITH YOUR CLASS: Get Well Card for a Member of the Class
Is anyone in your class sick or injured? Send a get well card from the class.

Valentine's Day Cards

February 14 is Valentine's Day. On this occasion, many people send cards, candy, or flowers to someone they love. Children often exchange valentines in school.

1 WRITE YOUR OWN: Valentine
Copy the verse below onto the card.

1. Roses are red,
   Violets are blue,
   Sugar is sweet
   And so are you.
2. *Choose one:*
   • Love forever
   • I love you
   • All my love
   • Love
3. *Choose one:*
   • *Your signature*
   • *Your nickname*
   • Your Secret Admirer

2 WITH YOUR CLASS: Valentine Verse
Make up your own valentine verse. Write it in your notebook; then copy it on the board.

Sympathy Cards

If a friend or relative has a death in the family, you may send a card to express your condolences.

1 WRITE YOUR OWN CARD: Sympathy Card
Fill in the blanks.

1. *Choose one:*
   • In this time of sadness, our prayers are with you.
   • I was so sorry to hear of your loss.
   • My thoughts are with you.
2. *Your signature*

(1)

(2)

2 WITH YOUR CLASS: In Sympathy
Does the phrase *in sympathy* have the same meaning in your native language as in English? What phrases are used in your native language to express condolences?

Holiday Greeting Cards

Holiday cards have different pictures, colors, and greetings for each holiday.

1 WITH YOUR CLASS: Holiday Card
Look at this card. What holiday is it for? Write a greeting on the card.

2 WITH YOUR CLASS: Holiday Chart

Divide into groups of three or four students. Fill in the chart below with more holidays. Write the colors, symbols, and greeting for each holiday. Compare your chart with other charts of the class.

Holiday	Colors	Symbols	Greeting
Valentine's Day	red	heart Cupid	Happy Valentine's Day

3 ON THE BOARD: Holiday Greetings in Other Languages

What holidays do you celebrate in your native culture? Make a list on the board of the holidays and write the greeting for each holiday.

Congratulations Telegram

Use a telegram to send your congratulations.

1   WITH YOUR CLASS: Vocabulary

Read this telegram with your class and add more words to the vocabulary list.

2   WRITE YOUR OWN: Congratulations Telegram

Complete this telegram.

(1)

(2)

(3)

western union								Telegram	
MSG. NO.	NO. WDS CL. OF SVC.	PD.-COLL.	CASH NO.	ACCOUNTING INFORMATION		DATE	FILING TIME		SENT TIME
							A.M. P.M.		A.M. P.M.

Send the following message, subject to the terms on back hereof, which are hereby agreed to

☐ OVER NIGHT TELEGRAM
UNLESS BOX ABOVE IS CHECKED THIS MESSAGE WILL BE SENT AS A TELEGRAM

TO

ADDRESS & TELEPHONE NO.

CITY – STATE & ZIP CODE

CONGRATULATIONS ON YOUR

SENDER'S TEL. NO.   (Area Code)   NAME & ADDRESS   (Zip Code)

W.U. 5210 (3/73)

1. *Name, address, and telephone of a friend* or *relative*
2. *Choose one:*
   - graduation
   - new baby
   - engagement
   - *other:* _____
   _____
   _____
3. *Your telephone number, name, and address*

3   ON THE BOARD: Congratulations in Other Languages

How do you say "congratulations" in your native language? Write the expression on the board.

Telegram form courtesy of Western Union Telegraph Co.

CHAPTER FOLLOW-UP

1   Which of the handwritten messages are not full sentences? Add the missing part of the sentence orally.

2   Can you send other greetings by telegram? Write a list of greetings on the board.

3   Condolences are the opposite of congratulations. What cards do you send to extend condolences? What cards do you send to extend congratulations?

4   Did you ever give flowers for an occasion? For what occasion? Did you include an enclosure card with the flowers? What did you write on it?

5   Do people write greetings on cakes in your native country? What greetings have you seen written on cakes in the United States?

6   Where can you buy greeting cards in your community? Go to the store and look at them. Can you recognize what occasions they are for? For what seasonal holiday can you buy cards now?

7   Skim this chapter and circle all new vocabulary words. Make a list on the board of the vocabulary you remember from this chapter.

Money
and Credit

Teacher's Notes

Student Objectives:
- *to learn to write amounts of money*
- *to practice writing amounts of money on checks and forms*
- *to become familiar with forms for banking and credit in the United States.*

Sequence

1   Tell the students not to write anything until the class has discussed each page.

2   Preview each page separately by reading the instructions to the class and looking over the form, check, or chart on the page together.

3   Ask the students to share their own experiences with money, banking, and credit as you preview each page.

4   On some pages, there are many new vocabulary words. Don't skip over them. Pick out the difficult vocabulary words and have the students circle the unfamiliar words in their books. Write the words on the board and ask the students to copy them in their notebooks. Then reinforce the vocabulary by using it repeatedly in talking about the writing assignments.

5   Share this additional information with the class:

Credit cards were first used in the United States during the 1920's when corporations, such as oil companies and hotel chains, started issuing them to their customers to use for delayed payment. After World War II, their use increased greatly. In 1950, The Diner's Club, Inc. introduced the first universal credit card, to be used with a variety of companies.

Credit unions began in the mid-1800's in Italy and Germany. In Quebec, Alphonse Desjardins started the first credit union in North America in 1900. In 1909, Manchester, New Hampshire was the first United States site of a credit union. In Boston, Massachusetts, Edward Filene, a merchant, strongly supported its growth during this period.

6   Have the students complete the exercises on the page. Note that the **Telegram Asking for Money** and the **Telegraphic Money Order,** and the **Application for a Loan** and **Cosigning a Loan** are to be completed simultaneously by partners.

Arabic Numerals and Cardinal Numbers

1 WITH YOUR CLASS: Uses of Arabic Numerals and Cardinal Numbers

Arabic numerals were first used in India. In English, Arabic numerals are used for writing money. In writing checks, *cardinal numbers* are also used. Where else are *Arabic numerals* and *cardinal numbers* used?

2 WITH A PARTNER: Writing Arabic Numerals

While your partner dictates the cardinal numbers on the chart, write the Arabic numeral in your notebook, then dictate the numbers to your partner.

Arabic Numeral	Cardinal Number		Cardinal Number
0	zero	30	thirty
1	one	40	forty
2	two	50	fifty
3	three	60	sixty
4	four	70	seventy
5	five	80	eighty
6	six	90	ninety
7	seven	100	one hundred
8	eight	101	one hundred one
9	nine	102	one hundred two
10	ten	200	two hundred
11	eleven	300	three hundred
12	twelve	400	four hundred
13	thirteen	500	five hundred
14	fourteen	600	six hundred
15	fifteen	700	seven hundred
16	sixteen	800	eight hundred
17	seventeen	900	nine hundred
18	eighteen	1,000	one thousand
19	nineteen	5,000	five thousand
20	twenty	10,000	ten thousand
21	twenty-one	50,000	fifty thousand
22	twenty-two	100,000	one hundred thousand
23	twenty-three	500,000	five hundred thousand
24	twenty-four	1,000,000	one million
25	twenty-five	10,000,000	ten million
26	twenty-six	100,000,000	one hundred million
27	twenty-seven	1,000,000,000	one billion
28	twenty-eight		
29	twenty-nine		

3 WITH YOUR PARTNER: Writing Cardinal Numbers

While your partner dictates the cardinal numbers on the chart, write them in your notebook. Then dictate the numbers to your partner.

Writing Amounts of Money

These are the symbols for money in the United States:

Word	¢	$
one cent (penny)	1¢	$ .01
a nickel	5¢	$ .05
a dime	10¢	$ .10
a quarter	25¢	$ .25
a half dollar	50¢	$ .50
a dollar	—	$ 1.00 ($ 1.—)
five dollars	—	$ 5.00 ($ 5.—)
ten dollars	—	$ 10.00 ($ 10.—)
twenty dollars	—	$ 20.00 ($ 20.—)
fifty dollars	—	$ 50.00 ($ 50.—)
one hundred dollars	—	$100.00 ($100.—)

1 WITH YOUR CLASS: Writing Money

Listen to your teacher read these amounts of money. Then write the amounts.

1. one dollar and ninety-nine cents $1.99
2. a dollar sixty-seven   _____
3. a dollar and a half   _____
4. two dollars and a quarter   _____
5. five dollars   _____
6. twenty-five cents   _____
7. five cents   _____
8. ten dollars and two cents   _____

Checking Account—Writing Checks

You can get money orders or cashier's checks from a bank to pay bills, or you can keep your money in a checking account and use it by simply writing a check.

1 ON THE BOARD: Pay to the Order Of

On the board, write a list of the names of places in your community where you may pay by check—for example, stores, utility companies, hospitals, charities, your school. Copy the list in your notebook.

2 WITH YOUR CLASS: Parts of a Check

Read the sample check below. Do you usually write the amounts of money on checks this way? What other ways are also correct? (Example: Forty eight and six/100——) What other ways can you write the date? Is it correct to print your signature? Who is this check for?

No. *276*

November 19, 19 *82* $\frac{53-88}{113}$

PAY TO THE ORDER OF *Bell Telephone Company* $ *48.06*

Forty eight dollars and six cents——————— DOLLARS

essexbank
ESSEX COUNTY, MASSACHUSETTS

3 WRITE YOUR OWN: Check for a Million Dollars

Pretend you are giving away a million dollars. Fill in this check and then sign it.

No. *130*

——————— 19 —— $\frac{53-88}{113}$

PAY TO THE ORDER OF ————————————— $ —

One million and no/100——————————— DOLLARS

essexbank
ESSEX COUNTY, MASSACHUSETTS

Checking Account—Recording

Keep track of your *transactions* by recording them in your checkbook.

1 WITH YOUR CLASS: Checkbook

Look at this sample page from a checkbook. How much money is in the account now? (What is the *balance*?)

Who was paid on 6/4? (*description of deposit*) How much was paid? (*amount of check*)

How much money was put into the checking account on 6/4? (*amount of deposit*)

PLEASE BE SURE TO **DEDUCT** ANY PER CHECK CHARGES OR SERVICE CHARGES THAT MAY APPLY TO YOUR ACCOUNT

CHECK NO.	DATE	CHECKS ISSUED TO OR DESCRIPTION OF DEPOSIT	(−) AMOUNT OF CHECK	√ T	(−) CHECK FEE (IF ANY)	(+) AMOUNT OF DEPOSIT	BALANCE
							223 00
411	6/4	TO/FOR Dr. G. Katz	17 50				17 50
							BAL 205 50
	6/4	TO/FOR deposit				63 00	63 —
							BAL 268 50
		TO/FOR					BAL
		TO/FOR					BAL
		TO/FOR					BAL
		TO/FOR					BAL

2 WRITE YOUR OWN: Check to a Utility Company or Store

Fill in this check to a utility company or a store. Sign it. Then record it on the checkbook page above. Subtract it from the balance. What is the new balance?

No. _____

_____ 19 ____   53-88 / 113

PAY TO THE ORDER OF _____ $ _____

_____ **DOLLARS**

essexbank
ESSEX COUNTY, MASSACHUSETTS

Savings Account and Credit Union—Saving Money

You can save money in a savings account in a *bank* or in a *credit union*. To open a bank account or to join a credit union, you must fill out a *signature card*.

1 WRITE YOUR OWN: Credit Union Signature Card

In credit unions, people save money together and get low-cost loans from the union savings. Members of a company credit union all work for the same company. Members of an ethnic credit union (Portuguese, Italian, etc.) all are either in the ethnic group or friends of the ethnic group. Fill out this signature card and sign it.

ACCOUNT	ACCT. NO.

I hereby make application for membership and agree to conform to the By-laws, Rules and Regulations

of **CAMBRIDGE PORTUGUESE** CREDIT UNION

SIGNATURE

Home
Address

Birthplace   Date of Birth

Employed by   Position

Address   Father's name
                           Mother's maiden name

Approved by   Occupation

S.S.   Date opened
No.   Form 380   21

2 WRITE YOUR OWN: Payroll Deduction Authorization

If there is a credit union where you work, your company can deposit part of your paycheck in the credit union savings plan. The credit union will invest the money and you will receive the dividends. Complete this form.

Circle and write inside the box the percentage you wish to save by Payroll Deduction.

SAVINGS PLAN DEDUCTIONS:

Basic
Payroll   1% 2% 3% 4% 5% 6%
Deduction

Credit union signature card courtesy of Cambridge Portuguese Credit Union.

Depositing Money

1 WITH YOUR CLASS: Deposit Tickets

When you deposit money in a savings account or a checking account, you must fill out a deposit ticket. Fill out this deposit ticket to put a check for $125.63 and $50.00 cash in your savings account. What is your total deposit? Write it on the deposit ticket.

Name _____

Address _____

_____

DATE _____ 19_____

DEPOSIT TICKET

CURRENCY		
COIN		
TOTAL CHECKS		
TOTAL		

A Z ••• 0 0 6 8 ••• 1

ACCOUNT NUMBER

2 WRITE YOUR OWN: Endorsing a Check

You must *endorse* a check before you can deposit it in a savings or checking account. *Endorse* means write your signature on the back of the check. Endorse this check.

Withdrawing Money

1 WRITE YOUR OWN: Withdrawal Voucher—Savings Account

Read this withdrawal voucher with your class. Then fill it out to take out one hundred dollars from your savings account.

WITHDRAWAL   For Use in Banking Room Only   Pass Book No..........................

Received from ATLANTIC SAVINGS BANK

....DOLLARS

PLEASE WRITE AMOUNT IN WORDS

SIGN
HERE...

ADDRESS..

DOLLARS	CENTS
$	

100M-11/80   Check #.............   Payable to:...

2 WRITE YOUR OWN: A Check to Withdraw Money— Checking Account

Fill in this check to withdraw any amount of money from your checking account. After *Pay to the Order of,* write *Cash* or write your name. Sign the check. (You must endorse a check to withdraw money from your account.)

No. _____

_____ 19____   53-88
                            113

PAY
TO THE
ORDER OF_____ $_____

_____ DOLLARS

essexbank
ESSEX COUNTY, MASSACHUSETTS

_____

Telegram Asking for Money

1 **WITH YOUR PARTNER:** Write a Telegram Asking for Money

Complete this telegram to your partner. Exchange your telegram with your partner and send the money in Exercise 2 on the next page.

```
┌─────────────────────────────────────────────────────────────────┐
│  ⊔⊔⊔                                          Telegram             │
│  western union                                                     │
│ MSG. NO. │CL. OF SVC.│PD.-COLL.│CASH NO.│ ACCOUNTING INFORMATION │DATE│ FILING TIME │ SENT TIME │
│          │           │         │        │                        │    │    A.M.     │   A.M.    │
│          │           │         │        │                        │    │    P.M.     │   P.M.    │
│                                                                   │
│ Send the following message, subject to the terms on back hereof, which are hereby agreed to  ☐ OVER NIGHT TELEGRAM │
│ TO                                                       UNLESS BOX ABOVE IS CHECKED THIS │
│                                                         MESSAGE WILL BE SENT AS A TELEGRAM │
│ ADDRESS & TELEPHONE NO.                                            │
│ CITY – STATE & ZIP CODE                                            │
│     Please send                                                   │
│                                                                   │
│                                                                   │
│                                                                   │
│                                                                   │
│                                                                   │
│ SENDER'S TEL. NO.            NAME & ADDRESS                        │
│          (Area Code)                              (Zip Code )      │
│ W.U. 5210 (3/73)                                                  │
└─────────────────────────────────────────────────────────────────┘
```

(1)
(2)
(3)
(4)
(5)

1. *Your partner's name and address and telephone number*

2. *Choose one:*
   - $100.00
   - $500.00
   - $5,000.00
   - *other:* _____

3. *Choose one:*
   - Almost broke.
   - Must meet payments.
   - Out of money.

4. *Choose one:*
   - Appreciate your help.
   - Many thanks.
   - Thanks very much.

5. *Your telephone number, name, and address*

Telegram form courtesy of Western Union Telegraph Co.

Telegraphic Money Order

It is possible to send money by mail if you write a check. You can send money faster via either a *cable* or a *telegraphic money order.* To cable money, you do not have to write anything. Your bank can send wire transfers (money cables) from your account. To telegraph money, you must fill out a Telegraphic Money Order.

1 ON THE BOARD: Test Questions

Read this telegraphic money order with your class. On the board, make a list of possible *test questions.* A *test question* should be one that only the person receiving the money can answer (for example: What is your mother's maiden name? Or: What is your dog's name?)

2 WITH YOUR PARTNER: Telegraphing Money

Send the money your partner requested in the telegram on the preceding page. Write a test question that only your partner can answer. Put the answer in parentheses. Write a special message to your partner.

Telegraphic Money Order Application

western union

SENDING DATA	CLASS TYPE	OFFICE	WORD COUNT	DATE AND FILING TIME	CLERKS INIT. AND ACCTG. INFORMATION	$	AMT.
							FEE
						S	TOLLS
							RP MGM
MOD		940	=			E	TAX
	DO NOT WRITE ABOVE THIS LINE						TOTAL

PAY AMOUNT:_____ /100 DOLLARS (_____) =
FIGURES   CAU OR VIG

TO:_____ = REPORT PAYMENT BY MAILGRAM YES☐ NO☐ =
(ADDITIONAL CHARGE)

TEST QUESTION:_____ TELEPHONE NO._____ =
STREET ADDRESS
AND APT. NUMBER:_____ CITY:_____ STATE:____ ZIP:____ =

SENDER'S NAME:_____ =
SENDER'S STREET
ADDRESS AND APT. NO.:_____ CITY:_____ STATE:____ ZIP:____
(IF REPORT PAYMENT REQUESTED)

MESSAGE:_____ = MOD =

EOM (_____ / _____ / _____ / CS) . X-OFF
(SENDER'S NAME)   (ADDRESS)   (CITY-STATE-ZIP)

● Unless signed below the Telegraph Company is directed to pay this money order at my risk to such person as its paying agent believes to be the above named payee, personal identification being waived. Foreign money orders excepted.

W.U. 72
(R12-77)

II⁰087940891II 66   (TELEPHONE NO.)

Telegraphic Money Order Application form courtesy of Western Union Telegraph Co.

Applying for a Credit Card

With a credit card, you can buy something now and pay for it later. Sometimes you must pay *interest* (additional money) for this privilege.

1 WRITE YOUR OWN: Credit Card Application

Read this credit card application with your class. Then fill it out for yourself.

Credit Account Application

NAME AND ADDRESS OF CREDIT APPLICANT—NAME IN WHICH ACCOUNT IS TO BE CARRIED **COURTESY TITLES ARE OPTIONAL** ☐ MR. ☐ MRS. ☐ MS. ☐ _____ PLEASE PRINT	SOC. SEC. NO. AGE
First Name Middle Initial Last Name Street Address City State Zip Code	NUMBER OF DEPENDENTS PHONE NO.

If applicant's spouse is authorized to buy on the account, print name here:

If others are authorized to buy on the account, print names here:
1   2

HOW LONG AT PRESENT ADDRESS	☐ OWN ☐ BOARD ☐ RENT	MONTHLY RENT OR MORTGAGE PAYMENTS

FORMER ADDRESS (IF LESS THAN 2 YEARS AT PRESENT ADDRESS)		HOW LONG

EMPLOYER

ADDRESS	CITY	STATE	ZIP

HOW LONG	OCCUPATION	NET EARNINGS ☐ MONTHLY ☐ WEEKLY

FORMER EMPLOYER (IF LESS THAN 1 YEAR WITH PRESENT EMPLOYER)	HOW LONG

OTHER INCOME IF ANY AMOUNT $	Note: "Alimony, child support or maintenance income need not be revealed if you do not wish to have it considered as a basis for paying this obligation."	SOURCE OF OTHER INCOME

NAME OF BANK		BANK ACCOUNT	☐ SAVINGS ☐ LOAN ☐ CHECKING
ADDRESS	CITY		

PREVIOUS ACCOUNT?	☐ YES ☐ NO	AT WHAT STORE?	
ACCOUNT NO.		IS ACCOUNT PAID IN FULL? ☐ YES ☐ NO	DATE FINAL PAYMENTS MADE

CREDIT REFERENCES

NAME AND ADDRESS

ACCOUNT NUMBER	BALANCE	MONTHLY PAYMENT

NAME AND ADDRESS

ACCOUNT NUMBER	BALANCE	MONTHLY PAYMENT

NAME OF RELATIVE OR PERSONAL REFERENCE OTHER THAN SPOUSE

ADDRESS

_____ is authorized to investigate my credit record and to verify my credit employment and income references and to report my performance of this agreement to proper persons and bureaus. A consumer report may be requested in connection with this application. If the application is approved, subsequent reports may be requested during the life of the account. You may ask to be informed of whether a consumer report was requested and if so, the name and address of the consumer reporting agency furnishing the report. If the application is approved, _____ is authorized to release credit card(s) in the name of the applicant for the applicant and those designated as authorized to buy on the account.

SIGNATURE **X** _____   DATE _____

NOTE: YOU WILL BE PROVIDED A COPY OF THE CREDIT ACCOUNT AGREEMENT TO KEEP UPON APPROVAL

2 WITH YOUR CLASS: Credit Cards

Do you have a credit card? Is it a special card for an oil company or a store? Is it a universal credit card? Bring it in to show the class and explain what you can use it for.

Credit Card—Finance Charge

When you buy on credit, the credit card company sends you a monthly bill. Every month in which you have a *balance,* a *finance charge* is added to the balance.

1 WITH YOUR CLASS: Credit Card Statement

Read this credit card statement with your class. The previous balance was $548.30. How much money was then paid to the credit card company? What was the amount for charges made during this period? How much is the finance charge added to the bill? What is the new balance owed to the credit card company?

✱ INDICATES POSTING DATE NOT TRANSACTION DATE

TO PAY INSTALMENTS PAY THIS AMOUNT OR MORE
(IF PAST DUE HAS BEEN PAID PAY AMOUNT UNDER CURRENT MINIMUM)

NUMBER OF DAYS IN PERIOD   31

TO PAY YOUR ACCOUNT IN FULL REMIT THIS AMOUNT

PAST DUE	CURRENT MINIMUM	TOTAL MINIMUM DUE
	3200	3200

PREVIOUS BALANCE	TOTAL CREDITS THIS PERIOD	TOTAL DEBITS THIS PERIOD	FINANCE CHARGE	NEW BALANCE
54830	20000	46383	760	81973

TO AVOID ADDITIONAL **FINANCE CHARGES** PAYMENT OF NEW BALANCE MUST BE RECEIVED BY US BY   05/01/80

THE **FINANCE CHARGE** WAS COMPUTED SOLELY BY APPLYING THE FOLLOWING RATES TO THE AVERAGE DAILY BALANCE OF   **$509.60**

RANGE OF BALANCE(S) TO WHICH RATES APPLY		**ANNUAL PERCENTAGE RATE**	MONTHLY PERIODIC RATE
TO	500	18.000%	1.500%
OVER	500	12.000%	1.000%

YOU MAY CALL   IF YOU HAVE
ANY QUESTIONS CONCERNING THIS STATEMENT.

R-5003 REV. 3/79

2 WRITE YOUR OWN: Pay a Credit Card Bill

Fill in this check to pay the total minimum on the bill above.

No. _____

_____ 19 ___   53-88 / 113

PAY TO THE ORDER OF _____ $ _____

_____ DOLLARS

essexbank
ESSEX COUNTY, MASSACHUSETTS

_____

Applying for a Loan

Banks, credit unions, and finance companies can lend you money. Before they lend the money, they will check your credit to see if you are a good *credit risk*.

1 WITH YOUR CLASS: Vocabulary

Read the loan application on the opposite page with your class and discuss the vocabulary on the form.

2 ON THE BOARD: Provident Purposes

Write a list on the board of good reasons for taking out a loan.

3 ON THE BOARD: Security for a Loan

Write a list on the board of your property that you could use to secure a loan. (Example: your car)

4 WRITE YOUR OWN: Loan Application

Decide what you want to borrow money for. Fill out the loan application below.

APPLICATION FOR LOAN

Acct. No.: _____

I hereby apply for a loan of _____ dollars, for a period

of _____ to be repaid in ☐ Weekly ☐ Bi-Weekly installments of _____ dollars each.

I desire this loan for the following provident purpose: _____

_____

Security: _____

NAME - LAST	FIRST	MIDDLE	SOCIAL SECURITY NO.	DATE
ADDRESS	CITY	STATE	ZIP	YEARS AT PRESENT ADDRESS
HOME PHONE NO.	RESIDENCE ☐ Renting ☐ Buying	☐ Live with Parents ☐ Other (Specify) _____		NO. DEPENDENTS

LIABILITY TO OTHERS	BALANCE DUE	ACCOUNT OR CHARGE CARD NO.	OPEN ACCT.	Revolving	Installments

I am not indebted to any other credit union, bank or loan agency, either as maker or endorser, or others, except as stated above. The statements herein are made for the purpose of obtaining the loan, and are true.

DATE: _____ SIGNATURE: _____

All loan applications will be judged upon our fair evaluation of the individual applicant's credit history, steady employment or other source of income, and ability to repay the loan amount, without regard to sex or marital status. Income from alimony, child support or maintenance payments need not be revealed if the applicant does not choose to disclose such income in applying for this loan.

Cosigning a Loan

A *cosigner* (co-maker) is often required for a large loan. When you *co-sign* (co-make) a loan for a friend or relative, you are responsible for repaying the money if your friend or relative cannot repay it.

1 WITH YOUR CLASS: Cosigner's Statement
Read this statement with your class. Discuss the vocabulary.

2 WITH A PARTNER: Cosigning
Cosign your partner's loan application from the preceding page. Then have your partner cosign your loan application.

CO-MAKER'S STATEMENT

NAME	DATE OF BIRTH:

ADDRESS	SOCIAL SECURITY NO.:

	CITY	ZIP CODE	PHONE NO.

MARRIED ☐ SINGLE ☐ OTHER ☐	NAME OF WIFE/HUSBAND

EMPLOYER	YEARS HERE	PHONE NO.

ADDRESS	CITY	STATE

POSITION	INCOME (GROSS)	PER	WEEK / MONTH	(NET)

YRS AT PRESENT ADDRESS	OWN HOME?	RENT?	ARE YOU RELATED IN ANY MANNER TO THE MAKER OF THIS LOAN? ☐ YES ☐ NO	RELATIONSHIP

ARE YOU A CO-MAKER ON ANOTHER NOTE OR NOTES? ☐ YES ☐ NO	MY TOTAL INDEBTEDNESS IS $

I understand that in case of default of the maker of this loan I will be responsible for the full amount of principal and interest due.

DATE	SIGNED

Courtesy of Blue Cross and Blue Shield of Massachusetts, Inc.

Repaying a Loan

When you borrow money, you repay the money in *monthly installments.* The installment includes the finance charge on the loan. Sometimes you receive a book of monthly installment coupons. Every month you tear out a coupon and mail it with a check to the bank or loan company.

1 WRITE YOUR OWN: Paying a Monthly Installment

Imagine this is your monthly installment coupon for a new car. Read the coupon. Then write a check to the Bay Bank to pay the installment. Write your name and the *amount remitted* (the amount of the check). What is the penalty if you pay late? _____

No. 18	ACCOUNT NO. 10134766	DUE DATE May 15, 1982	AMOUNT $104.72

LATE CHARGE IF APPLICABLE → LATE CHARGE 5.00

AMOUNT REMITTED

Name: _____

Bay Bank/Middlesex

COUPON MUST ACCOMPANY PAYMENT

No. 113

_____ 19_____   53-235 / 113

PAY
TO THE
ORDER OF _____ $ [   ]

_____ DOLLARS

Bay Bank/Middlesex

memo _____   _____

CHAPTER FOLLOW-UP

1 How do you write *"six cents"* using Arabic numerals and symbols? *"one million dollars"*? *"a dollar and a half"*?

2 How much money did the class "send" by telegraphic money order?

3 What is a *"test question"*?

4 Why is a checking account useful? List the ways it is useful on the board.

5 What information do you record in your checkbook? When do you write a check?

6 What do you do when you receive a monthly checking account statement from the bank?

7 Why do you pay *interest* (a finance charge) on a loan or on credit card charges?

8 What credit unions are there in your community? What are the advantages of belonging to one?

9 What is your responsibility if you cosign a loan?

10 Should you sign or print your signature on checks or forms? What is a signature card? Look back at the signature page in the **Printing and Handwriting** chapter.

11 What is the difference between a credit card and a loan?

12 What is the difference between interest from a savings account and interest on a loan?

13 What new vocabulary do you remember from this chapter? Here is some additional vocabulary:

> overdraw
> balance
> "bounce" a check
> earned interest
> compounded quarterly
> bankrupt
> bad debt
> repossess
> collateral

6

Food:
Shopping
and
Preparation

Teacher's Notes

Student Objectives:
- to learn the vocabulary associated with food shopping and cooking (by writing recipes and shopping lists)
- to become familiar with ways of measuring weight, capacity and temperature in the United States.

Sequence

1 Tell the students not to write anything on the page until the class has discussed each page.

2
  a Preview **Favorite Sandwiches** and **Salads** by reading the recipes aloud, using the vocabulary from the list.
  b Preview the two shopping list pages and weight and capacity pages by discussing the value of bilingual shopping lists for learning vocabulary.
  c Preview the cooking pages by focusing on the illustrations of the thermometer and recipe card.

3 Discuss the page as a class.

4 For the first two pages of this chapter, list on the board the students' suggestions for other vocabulary.

5 Have the students complete the exercises in their books.

6 Have the students copy in their notebooks a sandwich recipe, a salad recipe, a dessert recipe, and any other recipes or vocabulary written on the board.

Favorite Sandwiches

1 WITH YOUR CLASS: Vocabulary

Add more words to the list.

2 WRITE YOUR OWN: Favorite Sandwich Recipes

Complete this simple recipe for a sandwich.

_____ (1)

Spread _____ (2)

on _____ (3).

Put on _____ (4)

and close the sandwich.

1. *Choose one:*
   - roast beef sandwich
   - peanut butter and jelly sandwich
   - tuna fish sandwich
   - bacon, lettuce, and tomato (BLT) sandwich
   - *other:* _____
2. *Choose one:*
   - mayonnaise
   - butter
   - margarine
   - mustard
   - ketchup
   - peanut butter
   - *other:* _____

3. *Choose one:*
   - 2 slices of rye bread
   - 2 slices of wheat bread
   - 1 split bun
   - *other:* _____
4. *Choose as many as you like:*
   - bologna
   - roast beef
   - tuna fish
   - bacon
   - tomato slices
   - lettuce
   - cheese
   - jelly
   - *other:* _____

3 ON THE BOARD: Sandwiches from Other Countries

Write a recipe on the board for a sandwich that people eat in your native country. Copy the recipe in your notebook.

Salads

1 WITH YOUR CLASS: Salad Ingredients
Do you know all these salad ingredients? Write a list of the vocabulary on this page and take it to the market. Find as many of these ingredients in the store as you can. Then tell the class what you found and what you didn't find.

2 WITH YOUR CLASS: Vocabulary
Add more words to the list.

3 WRITE YOUR OWN: Write a Garden Salad Recipe
Complete this recipe.

> ## TOSSED SALAD
>
> _____   _____
> into small pieces and put in bowl.
>   (1)   (2)
> Add _____
>   (3)
> _____.
> Garnish with _____.
>   (4)
> Serve with _____
>   (5)
> dressing.

1. *Choose one:*
   - tear
   - slice
   - shred
2. *Choose one or more:*
   - romaine lettuce
   - iceberg lettuce
   - cabbage
   - *other:* _____
     _____
     _____
3. *Choose as many as you like:*
   - cucumber slices
   - chopped green pepper
   - chopped scallions
   - *other:* _____
     _____

4. *Choose as many as you like:*
   - croutons
   - cheese
   - alfalfa sprouts
   - *other:* _____
     _____
     _____
5. *Choose one:*
   - Thousand Island
   - Italian
   - oil and vinegar
   - *other:* _____
     _____

Supermarket Shopping Lists

There are many kinds of packages in a supermarket. You must know the kinds of packages before you can write a shopping list.

1   WITH YOUR PARTNER: Types of Packages
Complete these lists. Write as many things as you can. Share your lists with the class.

Things you buy in boxes: *Things you buy in cans:*

_____   _____

_____   _____

_____   _____

_____   _____

2   ON THE BOARD: Other Packages
With your class write lists on the board of the kinds of things you buy in each of these packages: loaves, bunches, jars, bags (or sacks), bars, heads, bottles, tubes, six-packs. Copy the lists.

3   ON THE BOARD: Buying by Weights or Capacities
With your class, make lists on the board of things you buy by these weights or capacities:

a.   by the pound

b.   by the pint, quart, half gallon, or gallon

c.   by the dozen or half dozen

d.   by the peck or bushel
(Refer to the charts on pages 87–90 if you need to.)

4   WITH YOUR CLASS: Packages in Other Countries
Discuss with your class the differences between packages in the United States and in your native country. How are these things packaged in your native country?

rice

tomato paste

spices

meat

other: _____

_____

_____

5 WRITE YOUR OWN: Supermarket Shopping List
Finish this shopping list using the vocabulary from the preceding page.

2 loaves of rye bread
1 bunch _____
1 package_____
1 loaf _____
3 dozen _____
1 lb. _____
1 jar _____
2 cans _____
1 box _____
2 bottles _____

6 WITH YOUR PARTNERS: Comparing Shopping Lists
Write a shopping list of the things you and your family really buy at the supermarket. (If you don't know the English word, write it in your native language.)

Divide into groups of three or four students. Answer these questions:

1. Do you have any of the same things on your lists? Which things?

2. Did anyone write a bilingual shopping list? Which words?

3. Can you buy food from your native country in your market? Which food can you buy?

Report to the class about your group's discussion.

7 WITH A PARTNER: Dictate a Shopping List
Dictate your shopping list to a partner. Then write your partner's list from dictation. Check each other's lists.

Weight Conversion

1 ON THE BOARD: Converting Measurements of Weight

Use the Weight Conversion Chart below to convert the weights in these word problems. Read the chart and the word problems with your class. Then multiply on the board to find the correct answers. Copy the arithmetic in your book.

WEIGHT CONVERSION CHART		
When You Know:	**Multiply By:**	**To Find:**
ounces (oz) . . . × . . . . .28 . . . . = ...grams (g)
pounds (lb) . . . × . . . . .0.45 . . . . . = ...kilograms (kg)
short tons (T) (2000 lbs.) . × . . . . .0.9 . . . . . = ...tonnes (T)
grams (g) . . . . × . . . . .0.035 . . . . . = ...ounces (oz)
kilograms (kg) × . . . . .2.2 . . . . . . = ...pounds (lb)
tonnes (T) (metric tons) × . . . . .1.1 . . . . . . = ...short tons (T)

a. If you buy 5 pounds of flour, you are buying __2.25__ kilos. (5 × .45 = 2.25 kg.)

b. Two metric tons of coal are the same as _____ short tons. (_____ × _____ = _____)

c. When you buy an 18-ounce jar of peanut butter, how many grams does it weigh? _____ (_____ × _____ = _____)

d. The heaviest man in the world weighed 1069 pounds. How many kilos did he weigh? _____ (_____ × _____ = _____)

e. How many kilograms do you weigh? _____ How many pounds do you weigh? _____ (_____ × _____ = _____)

2 WRITE YOUR OWN: Converting Weights in Shopping

a. Look at the items you have at home from the supermarket. Which items are sold by weight? Write a list of them. Include the weight of each package. Share your list with the class.

b. Some packages show the weight in ounces and in grams because the United States is changing to the metric system. Write a list of three items from the supermarket with their weight in ounces and grams. Share your list with the class.

Weight Symbols and Equivalents

1 WITH YOUR CLASS: Symbols for Weight

Read this chart with your class. The symbols for ounces (oz) and pound (lb) come from the Latin words *uncia* and *libra pondo*.

WEIGHT SYMBOLS CHART

English System	*Metric System*
ounces = oz	grams = g
pounds = lb	kilograms = kg
short ton = T	metric ton = t (tonnes)

---

2 WRITE YOUR OWN: List of Equivalents

Fill in the correct symbols for the weight equivalents below. Check your answers with the class.

WEIGHT EQUIVALENCY CHART

a. One kilogram equals one thousand grams. _____

b. One metric ton equals one thousand kilograms. _____

c. One pound equals sixteen ounces. _____

d. One short ton equals two thousand pounds. _____

Volume Symbols And Conversion

1   WITH YOUR CLASS: Symbols for Volume (Converting English System to Metric System)

Read this chart of symbols for converting volume from the English system to the metric system. Notice there are two symbols for teaspoon and tablespoon.

VOLUME CONVERSION CHART (ENGLISH–METRIC)		
When You Know:	**Multiply By:**	**To Find:**
teaspoon (tsp, t) ....× .... 5 .... = ...		milliliters (ml)
tablespoon (tbsp, T) .....× .... 15 ...... = ...		milliliters (ml)
fluid ounces (fl. oz) ....× .... 30 ...... = ...		milliliters (ml)
cups (C) ....× .... 0.24 .... = ...		liters (l)
pints (pt) ....× .... 0.47 .... = ...		liters (l)
quarts (qt) ....× .... 95 ...... = ...		liters (l)
gallons (gal) ....× .... 3.8 .... = ...		liters (l)
bushels (bu) ....× .... 35 ...... = ...		liters (l)

2   WRITE YOUR OWN: List of Equivalents

Use the chart above. Write the correct symbols for these volume equivalents. Check your answers with the class.

VOLUME EQUIVALENCY CHART
a.   One tablespoon equals three teaspoons. _____
b.   One cup equals sixteen tablespoons. _____
c.   One pint equals two cups. _____
d.   One quart equals four cups. _____
e.   One gallon equals four quarts. _____
f.   One liter equals one thousand milliliters. _____

3 WITH YOUR CLASS: (Converting Metric System to English System)

Read this chart of symbols for converting volume from the metric system to the English system.

VOLUME CONVERSION CHART		
When You Know:	**Multiply By:**	**To Find**
milliliters (ml) .... × ...... 0.2 ...... =		...... teaspoons (tsp, t)
milliliters (ml) .... × ...... 0.6 ...... =		...... tablespoons (tbsp, T)
liters (l) .... × ...... 4.2 ...... =		...... cups (C)
liters (l) .... × ...... 2.1 ...... =		...... pints (pt)
liters (l) .... × ...... 1.06 ..... =		...... quarts (qt)
liters (l) .... × ...... 0.26 ..... =		...... gallons (gal)
liters (l) .... × ...... 0.03 ..... =		...... bushels (bu)

4 ON THE BOARD: Converting Volume

Use the Volume Conversion Charts to convert the volumes in the word problems below. First read the chart and the problems with your class. Then multiply on the board to find the correct answers. Copy the arithmetic in your book.

a. A recipe calls for 1 teaspoon of salt; that's ____5____ ml.
   (____1____ × ____5____ = ____5 ml____)

b. I need 3 cups of sugar to fill the sugar bowl. How many liters do I need?
   (_____ × _____ = _____)

c. When you pick 3 liters of strawberries, you have _____ pints.
   (_____ × _____ = _____)

d. Many doctors recommend drinking one liter of water a day. How many quarts is one liter? (_____ × _____ = _____)

e. Ten gallons of gasoline are approximately _____ liters.
   (_____ × _____ = _____)

f. In one liter of milk, there are _____ cups.
   (_____ × _____ = _____)

Recipes

1 WITH YOUR CLASS: Reading a Recipe

A *recipe* gives a list of ingredients and instructions for mixing and cooking. Read this recipe with your class. Notice the weight and volume measurements.

Chocolate Cheese Pie

Ingredients:
15 oz. cream cheese   1½ tsp. vanilla
2 eggs   ½ c. semi-sweet
½ c. sugar   chocolate chips

Mix all ingredients except chocolate until smooth. Pour into greased 9" pie plate. Melt chocolate. Drop by teaspoons into pie. Swirl. Bake at 325°F for 30 minutes.

---

2 WITH YOUR CLASS: Weight and Volume in Recipes

Look at the recipe for Chocolate Cheese Pie. Use the Weight and Volume Conversion Charts. Answer these questions with the class.

a. How many ounces of cream cheese does this recipe call for? (weight) _____ How many grams? _____

b. How many cups of sugar do you need? (volume) _____ How many liters? _____

c. How many liters of chocolate chips do you need? (volume) _____

d. How many milliliters of vanilla do you need? (volume) _____

3 WITH YOUR CLASS: International Recipes

Prepare your favorite recipe from your native country. Bring it to class to share. Write the recipe on a recipe card. Make an international recipe file with all the recipes from the class.

Temperature Conversion

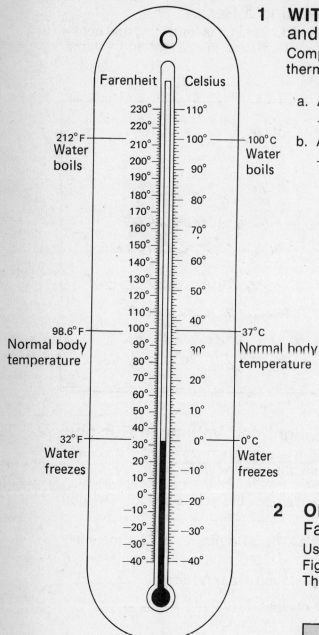

Farenheit   Celsius

230° — 110°
220°
212° F — 210° — 100° — 100° C
Water   Water
boils   200° — 90°   boils
190°
180° — 80°
170°
160° — 70°
150°
140° — 60°
130°
120° — 50°
110°
100° — 40°
98.6° F — 100° — 37° C
Normal body 90° — 30°   Normal body
temperature 80°   temperature
70° — 20°
60°
50° — 10°
40°
32° F — 30° — 0° — 0° C
Water   20°   Water
freezes 10° — −10°   freezes
0°
−10° — −20°
−20° — −30°
−30°
−40° — −40°

1 WITH YOUR CLASS: Comparing Fahrenheit and Celsius

Compare the Celsius and Fahrenheit temperatures on this thermometer.

a. At what temperature does water boil? _____ °C or _____ °F

b. At what temperature does water freeze? _____ °C or _____ °F

2 ON THE BOARD: Converting from Fahrenheit to Celsius

Use this formula to convert from Fahrenheit to Celsius. Figure out the word problems on the board. Then copy the arithmetic in your book.

FAHRENHEIT TO CELSIUS

$(°F - 32) \times 5/9 = °C$

Subtract 32 degrees from the Fahrenheit temperature. Then multiply by 5/9.

EXAMPLE: $(212°F - 32) = 180 \times 5/9 = 100°C$

---

a. The oven temperature to bake a cake is usually about 350°F or _____°C.

(_____°F − 32 = _____ × 5/9 = _____°C)

b. The oven temperature to broil meat is usually 550°F. How many degrees Celsius is it?

(_____°F − 32 = _____ × 5/9 = _____°C)

c. What is the temperature today in Fahrenheit? _____°F in Celsius? _____°C

(_____°F − 32 = _____ × 5/9 = _____°C)

d. Look back at the recipe page. The oven temperature for baking the Chocolate Cheese Pie is 325 °F. How many degrees Celsius is it?

(_____°F − 32 = _____ × 5/9 = _____°C)

3 ON THE BOARD: Converting from Celsius to Fahrenheit

Use this formula to convert from Celsius to Fahrenheit. Figure out the word problems on the board. Then copy the arithmetic in your book.

CELSIUS TO FAHRENHEIT

9/5°C + 32 = °F

Multiply the Celsius temperature by 9/5. Then add 32.

EXAMPLE: 9/5 × 100°C = 180° + 32° = 212°F

---

a. If the temperature of a room is 20°C, what is the temperature in Fahrenheit?

(9/5 × _____°C = _____ + 32 = _____°F)

b. What is the usual temperature in your native country in the summer?

_____°C or _____°F

(9/5 × _____°C = _____ + 32 = _____°F)

c. What is the usual winter temperature in your native country?

_____°C or _____°F

CHAPTER FOLLOW-UP

1 Do you know how to use the English system for the following:

    a food shopping
    b measuring ingredients for recipes
    c baking
    d broiling
    e frying
    f weather
    g body temperature

2 Where have you seen the metric system used in the United States?

3 Why are abbreviations used in shopping lists and recipes? What are some abbreviations you have seen?

4 What is a recipe? What does it include?

5 Read the following paragraph:

Metric units are a product of the French Revolution and became compulsory in France in 1840. There has been a dispute about using metric units in the United States since colonial times. In the nineteenth century, according to the National Institute of Education, some people in the United States called the metric system "atheistic." They thought the Anglo-Saxon system was "divinely ordained." In an attempt to convert the English system, President Ford signed the Metric Conversion Act of 1975.

6 Why is it convenient to use a shopping list? How will a shopping list in English make your shopping easier?

7 Write to the National Bureau of Standards, Washington, D.C. 20234 for an information booklet, *What About Metric*?

8 In the United States, many people shop for food once a week in the supermarket, using a shopping cart as they shop. They carry their groceries home in brown paper bags. Do people shop for food this way in your country? If not, what are the differences?

9 What other kinds of salads do you make besides the one shown on page 84? (gelatin, fruit, potato, macaroni, etc.) Write other salad recipes on the board.

10 Skim this chapter and circle all new vocabulary words. Make a list on the board of the vocabulary you remember from this chapter.

Consumer Needs

Teacher's Notes

Student Objective:
- to become familiar with the writing tasks associated with a variety of consumer needs.

Sequence

1   Tell the students not to fill in the blanks until the class has discussed the page.

2   Preview each page by reading the page title and looking over the illustrations together. Ask for student experiences with these situations.

3   Provide a model on the pages with blanks to fill in. Read the form or the list using the vocabulary given.

4   Discuss the meaning of all vocabulary words on each page.

5   Ask for suggestions for other vocabulary. Write the vocabulary words on the board and discuss them. Have the students write the words in their books.

6   Do the writing exercises on the page. After the students fill in the required information, always compare answers together. Answer any questions the students may have.

Free Offers

1 WITH YOUR CLASS: Free Offer Cards

Read these free offer cards with your class. If you mail them, what will you receive?

2 WRITE YOUR OWN: Filling In Free Offer Cards

Fill in this card. Print the information.

SEND ME A BOOK ABOUT:

☐ **Regular enlistment.**

☐ **Hometown service with the Marine Reserve.**

Mr.
Ms. _____
        PLEASE PRINT

Address _____

City _____

State _____ Zip _____

Telephone Number _____

Name of School _____

Last grade completed _____

Date of Birth   Month   Day   Year

MGSPA10017
Sport

---

3 WITH YOUR CLASS: Other Free Offers

You can find free offer cards in magazines, newspapers and supermarkets. Find some and share them with your class. Are the offers really free? Read the fine print. Practice filling out the cards.

Subscriptions

1   **WITH YOUR CLASS:**   Subscription cards
Read this subscription card. What does it offer? How much does the subscription cost?

2   **WRITE YOUR OWN:**   Filling in a Subscription Card
Fill in this card. Print the information.

3   **ON THE BOARD:**   Other Subscriptions
Make a list on the board of newspapers and magazines that you can subscribe to. What else can you subscribe to?

Sports Illustrated Bonus Offer sample courtesy of *Sports Illustrated* © 1981 Time Inc.

Ads for Household Items

If you want to buy or sell household items, you may want to use the *classified advertising section* of a local newspaper.

1 WITH YOUR CLASS: Do-It-Yourself Coupon for Household Items

Sometimes newspapers provide *coupons* for your convenience. The coupon makes it easier for you to write an advertisement for the newspaper. Read through this advertisement coupon with your class. Discuss the vocabulary. Add more vocabulary to the list.

2 WRITE YOUR OWN: Filling In a Do-It-Yourself Coupon

Complete the ad.

I want my classified to run under the following category:

☐ Personals   ☐ Bldg. Contractors   ☐ Wanted to Buy   ☐ Instructions
☐ For Sale   ☐ Real Estate   ☐ Pets   ☐ Boats
☐ Help Wanted   ☐ For Rent   ☐ Lost Passbooks   ☐ Used Cars
☐ Services   ☐ Wanted To Rent   ☐ Lost & Found   ☐ Yard Sales
                                                                   ☐ Other . . . . . .

Use the five convenient lines below to write your ad. Then compute the cost by adding up the number of words and multiplying times the appropriate cost per word: **(20-word minimum)**

Ad to run 3 times — 14¢ per word x 3. Minimum $8.40
Ad to run 2 times — 16¢ per word x 2. Minimum $6.40
Ad to run once — 17¢ per word. Minimum $3.40

*These rates do not apply to commercial automotive sales and real estate sales.

I want my ad to run ☐ once, ☐ twice, ☐ three times. (Check One)
I enclose check for $_____ to cover the cost of my ad.

(1)
(2)
(3)
(4)

NORTH SHORE: SUNDAY
Do-it-yourself
Ad coupon

Name.   Address
City.   Phone

1. *Choose one:*
   • Moving.
   • Forced to sell.
   • For sale:
   • Must sell:
   • *other:* _____
   _____

2. *Choose what you want to sell:*
   • bed $45.
   • couch $50.
   • dresser $100.
   • television (15 in.) $50.
   • *other:* _____
   _____
   _____

3. *Choose one:*
   • All in good shape
   • Excellent condition
   • *other:* _____
   _____

4. *Your telephone number*

Do-It-Yourself coupon courtesy of *North Shore: Sunday.*

3   WITH A PARTNER: Write Your Own Ad

With your partner, write an ad to sell some household items you have in your house now. Write it on the board and explain it to the class.

4   WITH A PARTNER: Ad for a Yard Sale

A sale that takes place in a private home has many names: *patio sale, yard sale, garage sale.* The sale is open to the public. Write an ad with your partner for a yard sale. Write some of the things you would sell, the date, and the time of the sale.

Ads for Used Cars

If you want to buy or sell a car, ads in a local newspaper can help you.

1 ON THE BOARD: Abbreviations in Advertisements

Newspaper ads are short because short ads cost less money. Read the ads for used cars below. Make a list on the board of abbreviations from these ads. What does each abbreviation mean? (Notice that abbreviations in ads do not always use periods.)

A CARS sale $395 up. Fords, Chevys, Plyms. & other small cars.

BUICK Skylark 1978, H.B. 6 cyl. auto., air, #273. $4250. WOBURN V.W., 196 Lexington St., Woburn.

BUICK Skylark, 1973, 49K mi., 4 dr., 8 track, slight rust, runs strong. $695. ECK'S AUTO.

BUICK, 1976, 1 owner Electra LTD, 4 dr., all power, leather inter., well cared for, Ask.$2900.

BUICK Regal, 1976, V6, a/c, p.b., p.s., AM/FM stereo, excel. car. $3595 or B.O.

CADILLAC Seville, 1981, brand new, never reg. no mi., twilight blue, loaded List price $25,000, will sell $21,000. Would consider trade plus cash.

CADILLAC, Eldorado, 1977, sunrf., exc. $5000/b.o.

HONDA Accord LX 2 dr. 1979, bronze, loaded, 5 spd., #291. $6250. WOBURN V.W., 196 Lexington St., Woburn.

HONDA Accord 2 dr. 1977, 5 spd., gold, very clean, #250. $4250. WOBURN V.W., 196 Lexington St., Woburn.

HONDA Civic, 1979, excel. cond., std. trans., am-fm radio, $4500. Call Laura

HONDA, Civic, 1980, mint cond.. low mi. $4500 or bo.

LANCIA 1800, 1976, blue, low mi., new tires, mint cond. $3500.

MAZDA 1979 RX7GS, 16K mi., stereo, 5 speed. $7900.

MERCEDES, 1971, 280SL, auto. trans., factory air cond., mech. excel., 2 tops, Convertible top new excel. cond., must be seen, ask. $14,500. Call btwn. 7&9 p.m.

FORD Granada 2 dr. ESS, 1979, 6 cyl. auto., 23,000 mi. emerald green, extra clean, #218. $4750. WOBURN V.W., 196 Lexington St., Woburn,

FORD, Mustang, '80, 6800 mi., factory warrantv. 4 cyl. 5 spd. $5600.

FORD T-Bird, 1979, low mi., P/S, P/B, stereo cass., ask. $5500.

LINCOLN, '76 Town Car, silver, Beautiful! auto., power, ac., $2900.

MERCURY Lynx 1981 GS wagon 4 cyl., auto, ps, am-fm stereo, r. window defrost, woodgrain siding, 1800 mi., mint cond, $6895 or bo.

OLDSMOBILE, Cutlass Supreme, 1977, 2 dr., std., 6 cyl., orig. 31K mi. $2900.

OLDS Starfire 1980, 4 cyl. auto., ps., 12,000 mi. #285. $4950. WOBURN V.W., 196 Lexington St., Woburn,

2 WITH YOUR PARTNERS: Write an Ad to Sell a Used Car

Do any students in your group own a car? Develop an ad to sell a car owned by one student. Write your ad on the board and explain it to the class.

Classified ads courtesy of *The Boston Globe*.

Ads for Services and Repairs

Use the classified section to look for words such as repairing, painting, odd jobs, typing, or translating, or to look for someone to do this work for you.

1 WITH YOUR CLASS: Reading Ads for Services and Repairs

Read these ads with your class and write the names of the services next to each ad.

TREES CUT DOWN CHEAP
$99 to $149. Call anytime, prof. tree cutters.

ARTHUR Painting Co. Ext. & inter. painting & paper hanging.

BATH TUBS resurfaced on loc. colors. $180. guar. Lectroglaz.

C & D Improvements, carpentry, roofing, int. & ext. painting. Free estimates, very reasonable. Call Dennis aft. 5:30.

FLOORS, Hdwd. Sanded-laid-refin-compl-remod. Most qual. lowest poss. rate. Comm'l-res. Free est. NORTHERN FINISHING INC.

HOT TOP, drives, walks, new or resurface, seal coating, experienced.

INT-EXT painting. Compl-remod. Most qual. ai lowest poss-rate. Comm'l-res. Free est. NORTHERN FINISHING INC.

I will assemble anything in my home.

J&J LANDSCAPING, tree service and spring cleaning.

LIC. CARPENTRY, gutter, kitchen, porches & painting. Int. & ext.

MASONRY, Tiles, Concrete. Carpentry-kitchens remod. Solar projects.

TRUCKING, Cleaning yds, cellars,etc.brush unwanted junk remov.

2 WRITE YOUR OWN: Writing an Ad for Services or Repairs

Fill in this ad for a service that you could perform.

```
_____ by local
              (1)

person. Very
                     (2)

              Call
(3)                        (4)
```

1. *Choose one:*
   - Typing
   - Housepainting
   - Moving
   - Yard work
   - Translating
   - *other:* _____
   _____

2. *Choose one, two, or three:*
   - dependable
   - careful work
   - *other:* _____

3. Choose one, two or three:
   - Minimum wage
   - Only $_____
   - $_____/hour
   - *other:* _____

4. *Your telephone number*

Home Repairs: Tools and Supplies

1 WITH YOUR CLASS: Jobs around the House

Write the name of the tool or kind of supplies you need to finish these jobs at home. If you use other tools or supplies for these jobs, add them to the list.

Job	*Tools and Supplies*
Measure your room.	wrench
Tighten the bolt on your bicycle's handlebars.	flashlight and batteries
Glue together pieces of a plate you dropped.	glue
Replace a washer on a leaky faucet. (You don't know the size.)	folding rule or steel tape
Read your water meter in the dark basement.	assorted faucet washers
Hang a picture on the wall.	hammer and nails
Tighten a Phillips screw.	saw
Cut some wood for the fireplace.	Phillips screwdriver

Job	Tools and Supplies
Drill a hole in the wall.	penknife
_____	
Cut the insulation off an electrical wire because you are replacing a plug.	pair of pliers
_____	
	fuse
Replace a fuse that "blew" because the electrical system was overloaded.	
	electric drill
_____	
Unclog a sink drain.	
	lubricating oil
_____	
Fix a door that makes noise when you open and close it.	
	screwdriver
_____	
Twist two electrical wires together.	
	plunger
_____	
	other: _____
	_____
	_____
	_____
	_____
	_____
	_____

2 WRITE YOUR OWN: Toolbox Supplies
Write a list of the tools and supplies you have at home now.

TOOLBOX

_____

_____

_____

_____

_____

_____

_____

_____

_____

_____

_____

_____

3 WITH YOUR PARTNERS: Add to Your List
Divide into groups of three or four students. Compare your list with the other students' lists. Add any important tools or home repair supplies missing from your list.

Sewing Needs

1 ON THE BOARD: Sewing Necessities

Which of these items do you have at home for sewing? Make a class list of recommended items for a sewing basket or sewing box.

spools of thread   pinking shears

needles   hem tape

scissors   *other:* _____

thimble   _____

pins   _____

safety pins   _____

tape measure   _____

buttons   _____

2 WRITE YOUR OWN: Shopping Lists for a Fabric Store

Make lists of things you would buy to:

a. Sew on a button

b. Patch a pair of pants

c. Mend a hem

Fabric Store List

Length Symbols and Equivalents

1 WITH YOUR CLASS: Symbols for Length

Read this chart with your class. Notice there are two symbols for inches and two symbols for feet.

LENGTH SYMBOLS CHART

English System

inches = in. = ″
feet = ft. = ′

Metric System

millimeters = mm
centimeters = cm
meters = m

---

2 WRITE YOUR OWN: List of Equivalents

Fill in the correct symbols for length equivalents below. Check your answers with the class.

LENGTH EQUIVALENCY CHART

a. One foot equals twelve inches. _____

b One yard equals three feet. _____

c. One centimeter equals one hundred millimeters.

_____

_____

Length Conversion

1. **ON THE BOARD:** Converting Measurements of Length
Use the Length Conversion Chart to convert distances in the word problems below. First read the chart and the word problems with your class. Then multiply on the board to find the correct answers. Copy the arithmetic in your book.

LENGTH CONVERSION CHART

When You Know:		Multiply By:	To Find:
inches (in.)	x	25	millimeters (mm)
inches (in.)	x	2.5	centimeters (cm)
feet (ft.)	x	30	centimeters (cm)
feet (ft.)	x	0.3	meters (m)
yards	x	0.9	meters (m)
millimeters	x	0.04	inches (in.)
centimeters	x	0.4	inches (in.)
centimeters	x	0.033	feet (ft.)
meters	x	3.3	feet
meters	x	1.1	yards

a. If I want to buy 3 meters of cloth, I want to buy _____ yards.

(___3___ x ___1.1___ = _3.3 yd_)

b. If you buy a 6′ long board, what is its length in meters?

(_____ x _____ = _____)

c. A piece of paper for a business letter is 8½″ × 11″. What is its size in centimeters?

(_____ x _____ = _____)

(_____ x _____ = _____) (_____ x _____)

d. The tallest person in the world, according to the *Guinness Book of World Records*, is 8ft. 2 in. tall. How tall is he in centimeters?

(_____ x _____ = _____)
How tall is he in meters?

(_____ x _____ = _____)

e. What is your height in meters? _____ in centimeters? _____

in feet? (_____ x _____ = _____)

in inches? (_____ x _____ = _____)

Patient's Information Form

When you go to a doctor's office for the first time, you may have to fill out a form like the one below.

1   WRITE YOUR OWN: Patient Information Form
Complete this form.

PATIENT'S INFORMATION FORM

Name: _____

Address: _____

Telephone: _____ Birthdate: ___/___/___ Age: _____

Social Security Number: _____-_____-_____

Employer: _____ Occupation: _____

Address: _____ Phone: _____

Marital Status: Single ____ Married ____ Divorced ____ Widowed ____

Person responsible for bill: _____ Relationship: _____

Address: _____

Do you have medical insurance? Yes _____ No _____

Are you currently taking any medication? Please list: _____

_____

Are you allergic to any medication? Please list: _____

_____

Reason for visit: _____

Who referred you to this office? _____

I understand that I am fully responsible for all charges made for any professional service rendered:

_____   _____
           date   signature

Buying Insurance

You must fill out a health statement when you buy a medical or life insurance policy.

1 WITH YOUR CLASS: Medical Insurance Application

Discuss the vocabulary on this application with your class. Fill in the application.

HEALTH STATEMENT APPLICATION
(PLEASE PRINT)

CHECK THE COVERAGE YOU ARE APPLYING FOR:
- ☐ Major Medical Plan 1
- ☐ Optional Plan 2

☐ I am applying for new membership.
☐ I am applying to increase my coverage.

Refer to page 9 "Instructions for Application" to determine your eligibility for Individual or Family coverage.
☐ Family   ☐ Individual

If you are now, or have been in the past year, a member of Blue Cross and Blue Shield of Massachusetts, please give your IDENTIFICATION NUMBER.

Identification Number

1 Applicant's Name   Last_____ First_____ Initial____
Home Address   Street _____
City_____ State_____ Zip_____
Check One: ☐ Single   ☐ Married   ☐ Widowed   ☐ Divorced   ☐ Legally Separated
Employer's Company Name_____
Address _____

SOC. SEC. NO. _____
Date of Birth _____
Sex   ☐ Male   ☐ Female
Height _____   Weight _____

2 Spouse's Name _____
Date of Birth _____ Height_____ Weight_____
3 Number of unmarried children under nineteen years of age _____

4 Have you or any member of your family **to be covered** had any of the following for which you have received treatment in the last three years? You must print either "YES" or "NO" for each item. If "YES," UNDERLINE THE SPECIFIC AILMENTS.

Print YES or NO

A Bronchitis, asthma, tuberculosis, other respiratory infections . . . . _____
B Cysts, tumors, cancer, other growths . . . . _____
C Goiter, thyroid, other throat conditions . . . . _____
D High blood pressure, low blood pressure, heart trouble, anemia . . . . _____
E Eye, ear, nasal conditions . . . . _____
F Mental disorders, alcoholism, drug addiction . . . . . . _____
G Stomach or bowel conditions . . . . _____

Print YES or NO

H Epilepsy or conditions of nervous system . . . . _____
I Hemorrhoids, rectal ailments, varicose veins . . . . _____
J Gallstones, gall bladder, or liver conditions . . . . _____
K Kidney stones, kidney, other urinary conditions . . . . . _____
L Bladder or prostate condition . . . . _____
M Arthritis, bursitis, rheumatism, bone conditions . . . . _____
N Gynecological conditions . . . . _____
O Hernia, back condition, or bodily deformity . . . . _____
P Diabetes . . . . _____

5 Have you or any member of your family **to be covered** had any symptoms of disease or other ailments or injuries in the last three years for which you have consulted a physician or psychologist?   ☐ YES   ☐ NO

6 Do you or any member of your family **to be covered** under this policy need to see a physician or psychologist or need hospital care for any condition that presently exists? (For pregnancy, please indicate expected delivery date.)   ☐ YES   ☐ NO

7 If you have answered "YES" to questions 4, 5 or 6, indicate the necessary information requested below. (Attach additional sheet if necessary.)

Patient's Name _____
Diagnosis and Treatment_____ Date_____
Physician's Name and Address _____
Hospital Name and Address _____

Patient's Name _____
Diagnosis and Treatment_____ Date_____
Physician's Name and Address _____
Hospital Name and Address _____

Health statement application courtesy of Blue Cross and Blue Shield of Massachusetts, Inc.

First Aid and Medical Supplies

1 WITH YOUR CLASS: Home Remedies

Read this list of common ailments and medical supplies. Match the name of the *home remedy* you would use for each ailment. If you use other supplies, add them to the list.

Ailment	Medical Supplies
sore throat _____	aspirin
fever _____	facial tissue
headache _____	cough medicine
stomachache _____	antacid
constipation _____	milk of magnesia
diarrhea _____	baking soda
cough _____	chamomile tea
toothache _____	honey
earache _____	*other:* _____
sore mouth (canker) _____	_____
other: _____	_____

2 ON THE BOARD: Cold Remedies in Other Countries

What do people do for a cold in your native country? On the board, make a list of *cold remedies* from all the students' native countries.

3 WITH YOUR CLASS: First Aid Kit

A first aid kit is a box containing medical supplies for common injuries. Read these lists with your class and write the home remedy you would use for each injury. If you use other emergency supplies, add them to the list.

Injury	First Aid Kit
sprained ankle _____	antiseptic ointment
cut _____	hydrogen peroxide
scratch _____	gauze bandage
burn _____	adhesive tape
sting _____	Ace bandage
blister _____	*other:* _____
sliver _____	_____

CHAPTER FOLLOW-UP

1 Make a list on the board of the catalogue stores in your city. Bring in catalogues (Sears, Montgomery Ward, etc.). Look through the catalogues together. Practice filling in order blanks.

2 Bring in sale flyers. Discuss their purpose. Make a list of what you need to buy. Is everything really on sale? Discuss the vocabulary. (Examples: *reduced, great bargain, special purchase, discount*).

3 Bring in copies of the Lost and Found section of the newspaper. What has been lost in each case, and what must you do to contact the owner?

4 Make a list on the board of as many different kinds of stores as you can think of. Discuss with the class what you can buy in each of these stores. What other kinds of stores are there in your native country? How are they different from the stores where you live now?

5 Bring in other subscription cards, free offer cards, and insert cards. What do the cards offer? What are the terms of the agreement (for example, record clubs)? What must the consumer do or send? Is there a money-back guarantee? Practice filling out the cards.

6 Bring in actual ads for yard sales. Discuss them. If you know the locations, draw maps to get from the school to the sales.

7 Make a list of things you would buy if you had $100,000 to spend. Read your list to the class.

8 Skim this chapter and circle all new vocabulary words. Make a list on the board of the vocabulary you remember from this chapter.

Traveling

Teacher's Notes

Student Objectives:
- *to practice drawing maps for giving directions*
- *to become familiar with forms related to driving*
- *to practice other kinds of writing related to traveling.*

Sequence

1 Tell the students not to fill in the blanks until the class has discussed each page.

2 Suggestions for previewing specific pages:
   a **Drawing a Map:** discuss the practical uses of maps.
   b **Application for a Driver's License:** discuss the reasons for requiring a driver's license. Are the applications and rule manuals available in the students' native languages?
   c **Distance Symbols and Conversion:** Ask which system the students are accustomed to. There is additional information on the metric system in the **Chapter Follow-up** for Chapter 6.

3 To preview each page, look at the page title with the students. Find out what the page title means by looking at the illustration on each page. *Note:* **Accident Report Form** and **Friendly Letter about a Visit** are each two pages long. Preview both pages together.

4 After previewing each page where the students fill in the blanks, provide a model of each letter and telegram by reading the letter to the students, using the vocabulary from the list. Discuss the vocabulary on the forms. Write the students' suggestions for other vocabulary on the board. Have the students copy these words in their books.

5 Fill in the blanks. Be sure the choices fit together. For example, *It was raining. The road surface was dry* does not make sense.

6 Have the students copy the completed letters and postcard in their notebooks.

Distance Symbols and Conversion

1 WITH YOUR CLASS: Symbols for Distance

Read this chart of symbols for distance with your class. Then write the symbols for the italicized words in the sentences below. Check your answers with the class.

DISTANCE SYMBOLS CHART

English System	*Metric System*
mile = mi.	kilometer = km
miles per hour = mph	kilometers per hour = kph
miles per gallon = mpg	kilometers per liter = kpl

---

a. The speed limit on United States highways is *fifty-five miles per hour.*

_____ *55 mph* _____

b. *One mile* equals five thousand two hundred eighty feet.

_____

c. *One kilometer* equals one thousand meters.

_____

d. Small cars usually get better gas mileage, more *miles per gallon,* than large cars.

_____

2 ON THE BOARD: Converting Measurements of Distance

Use the Distance Conversion Chart to convert the distances in the word problems below. First read the chart and the word problems with your class. Then multiply on the board to find the correct answers. Copy the arithmetic in your book.

DISTANCE CONVERSION CHART

When You Know:	Multiply By:	To Find:
miles (m) . . . . × . . . . . . 1.6 . . . . . =		. . . . . . kilometers (km)
miles per hour (mph) . . . . × . . . . . . 1.6 . . . . . =		. . . . . . kilometers per hour (kph)
miles per gallon . . . . × . . . . . . 0.42 . . . . =		. . . . . . kilometers per liter (kpl)
kilometers (km) . . . . × . . . . . . 0.62 . . . . =		. . . . . . miles (m)
kilometers per hour . . . . . . × . . . . . . 0.62 . . . . =		. . . . . . miles per hour (mph)
kilometers per liter . . . . . . × . . . . . . 2.4 . . . . . =		. . . . . . miles per gallon (mpg)
(mpg)		
(kph)		
(kpl)		

a. It is 2915 miles from New York to Los Angeles. How many kilometers is it? _____

(_2915_ × _1.6_ = _4664 km_))

b. It is 11,832 kilometers from Buenos Aires, Argentina to Berlin, Germany. How many miles is it? _____

(_____ × _____ = _____)

c. The speed limit in the United States is 55 mph or _____ kph.

(_____ × _____ = _____)

d. Is there a speed limit in your native country? How many kilometers per hour is it? _____ How many miles per hour is it? _____

(_____ × _____ = _____)

e. Do you have a car? What is your gas mileage? (How many miles per gallon do you get? How many kilometers per liter?) _____

(_____ × _____ = _____)

Accident Report Form

If you are a driver involved in an accident, notify the police immediately. You will have to fill out an accident report form.

1 WITH YOUR CLASS: Diagram of a Car Accident

Read the description of a car accident on this accident report form. Discuss the diagram instructions. Then draw a diagram of the accident.

DIAGRAM

INDICATE ON THIS DIAGRAM WHAT HAPPENED

Use one of these outlines to sketch the scene of your accident, writing in street or highway names or numbers.

1. Number each vehicle and show direction of travel by arrow:
2. Use solid line to show path before accident ———; dotted line after accident. -----
3. Show pedestrian by:
4. Show railroad by:
5. Show distance and direction to landmarks; identify landmarks by name or number.
6. Indicate north by arrow, as:

INDICATE NORTH BY ARROW

Describe What Happened: (Refer to Vehicles by Number)

The accident occured at 11:30 a.m. It was raining hard. I was driving west on Main St. through the intersection of Main St. and Canal St. at 10 mph. The signal light at the intersection was green. A motorcycle was traveling south on Canal St., coming to the intersection. It skidded and hit the right rear fender of my car.

My speed immediately prior to the accident was approximately _____ m.p.h.

Signature of operator making report _____ Date _____

2 WITH YOUR CLASS: Completing an Accident Report Form

Complete the accident report for the accident you diagrammed.

NOTE: Mark all items which apply. The diagram and description of what happened (below) need not be completed if separate 8½ x 11 size sheet with same detailed information is attached. Please sign report in space provided below.

LOCATION

City or Town Where Accident Occurred

Nearest Mile Marker

Reserved for Registry

Street Name and/or Route Number

at intersection with _____ N. S. E. W. Of nearest intersection, bridge, mile marker, railroad.

or _____ feet

Other Landmarks:

Which direction was each vehicle traveling?

Vehicle No. 1 — N. S. E. W.
No. 2 — N. S. E. W.

54
1 ☐ On ramp from route _____
2 ☐ Off ramp from route _____
3 ☐ At rotary

55
1 ☐ Area built up
2 ☐ Area not built up

TYPE

56 Accident Involved Collision With:

1 ☐ Pedestrian
2 ☐ Motor Vehicle in Traffic
3 ☐ Motor Vehicle Parked
4 ☐ Railroad train
5 ☐ Ran off roadway hit fixed object _____ feet from road
6 ☐ Bicycle
7 ☐ Overturned in road
8 ☐ Ran off roadway — non-collision
9 ☐ Fixed object on shoulder, sidewalk or island
A ☐ Other

57 If collision involved two or more vehicles mark one of the following:

1 ☐ Rear end   2 ☐ Angle   3 ☐ Head on

SITUATION

What were vehicles doing prior to accident? Mark appropriate box.

Vehicle **58-60**	1	2		Vehicle	1	2		Vehicle	1	2
1 Making right turn			8	Skidding			F	Parked		
2 Making left turn			9	Slowing or stopping			G	Stalled or disabled		
3 Making U turn			A	Crossing median strip			H	Stalled or disabled with flasher on		
4 Going straight ahead			B	Driverless moving vehicle			J	In process of parking		
5 Passing on right			C	Backing			K	Entering or exiting from alley or driveway.		
6 Passing on left			D	Starting in traffic			L	Other		
7 Stop sign			E	Starting from parked position						

Where was pedestrian located at time of accident? Mark appropriate box.

X	**61**		X	
1	At intersection	7		Getting on/off vehicle
2	Within 300 feet of intersection	8		Working on vehicle
3	More than 300 feet from intersection	9		Working in street
4	Walking in street with traffic	A		Playing in street
5	Walking in street against traffic	B		Not in street
6	Standing in street	C		Other

CONDITIONS

62 X	Light Conditions	**63** X	Traffic Controls		X		**64** X	Weather Conditions	**65** X	Road Surface	**76** X	Road Conditions
1	Daylight	1	Stop sign	6		Railroad crossing gate	1	Clear	1	Dry	1	No Defects
2	Dawn or dusk	2	Yield sign	7		Railroad automatic signal	2	Foggy	2	Wet	2	Holes, ruts, bumps
3	Darkness — road lighted	3	Warning sign	8		Control device not working	3	Cloudy	3	Snowy	3	Foreign matter on surface
4	Darkness — road unlighted	4	Signal light	9		No control present	4	Rain	4	Icy	4	Defective shoulder
		5	Officer or flagman				5	Snow	5	Other	5	Road under construction
							6	Sleet			6	Other

COLLISION CONDITIONS

66 X		X		X		X		X	
1	Entered median	4	Hit guard rail	7	Hit signpost	A	Embankment	D	Stone wall
2	Crossed median	5	Hit curbing	8	Hit utility or light pole	B	Ditch	E	Other post
3	Hit median barrier	6	Hit abutment	9	Hit tree	C	Rock ledge	F	Bridge rail

Friendly Letter about a Visit

1 WITH YOUR CLASS: Vocabulary

Read this friendly letter with your class. Add more words to the vocabulary list.

2 WRITE YOUR OWN: Friendly Letter about a Visit

Complete this friendly letter.

_____ (1)

Dear _____ (2),

I'm so glad you can come for a visit. Let me know when you will be arriving. The weather will probably be _____ (3). Bring _____ (4) and _____ (4) with you so we can _____ (5).

I'm really looking forward to seeing you again.

_____ (6),

_____ (7)

1. *Today's date*
2. *Name of a friend or relative*
3. *Choose one:*
   - cold
   - hot
   - snowy
   - *other:* _____
   _____
4. *Choose two:*
   - warm clothes
   - a bathing suit
   - boots
   - *other:* _____
   _____
5. *Choose one:*
   - go to the beach
   - go sightseeing
   - go to the mountains
   - *other:* _____
   _____
   _____
6. *Choose one:*
   - Love
   - As ever
   - Always
   - *other:* _____
   _____
   _____
7. *Your signature*

3 WITH A PARTNER: A Visit with Your Partner

Using the vocabulary above, write a friendly letter to your partner. Imagine that your partner will visit you in your native country or in your favorite place, during your favorite season.

4 WITH A PARTNER: Answer to a Friendly Letter

Exchange friendly letters from Exercise 3 with your partner. Write an answer to your partner's friendly letter.

_____
(1)

Dear _____,
(2)

   Thanks for your letter. It will be good to see you again and to be in _____
(3)
in the _____. I
(4)
will be sure to bring
_____ and _____
(5)   (5)
so that we can _____
(6)
_____.

   I'll be arriving on _____
(7)
Flight 738 at 8:30 p.m. on
_____. See you
(8)
then.

_____,)
(9)
_____
(10)

1. *Today's date*
2. *Name of your partner*
3. *Name of your partner's native country*
4. *Choose one:*
   - summer
   - spring
   - winter
   - autumn
5. *The clothing your partner's letter mentioned*
6. *The activity in your partner's letter, #5*
7. *Name of an airline company*
8. *A date next month*
9. *Choose one:*
   - Love
   - Always
   - As ever
   - other: _____
   _____
   _____

10. *Your signature*

5 WITH A PARTNER: Friendly Letters

Write a friendly letter on any subject to a partner. Exchange letters and write an answer to your partner's letter.

Arrival Telegram

Telegrams carry short, urgent messages. You can inform someone quickly about your travel arrangements by telegram.

1 WITH YOUR CLASS: Arrival Telegram

Imagine you are going to visit a relative or friend. Complete the blanks in this telegram form.

western union	**Telegram**

MSG. NO.	NO. WDS. CL. OF SVC.	PD.-COLL.	CASH NO.	ACCOUNTING INFORMATION	DATE	FILING TIME	SENT TIME
						A.M. / P.M.	A.M. / P.M.

Send the following message, subject to the terms on back hereof, which are hereby agreed to

☐ OVER NIGHT TELEGRAM
UNLESS BOX ABOVE IS CHECKED THIS
MESSAGE WILL BE SENT AS A TELEGRAM

TO

(1) ADDRESS & TELEPHONE NO.

CITY — STATE & ZIP CODE

(2) *Coming on*
(3) *Will arrive*
(4)
(5)
(6)

(7) SENDER'S TEL. NO.   NAME & ADDRESS
    (Area Code)   (Zip Code)

W.U. 5210 (3/73)

1. *Name, address, and telephone number of your friend or relative*

2. *Choose one:*
   - *Name of an airline*
   - *Name of a bus company*
   - *Name of a train*

3. *Choose one:*
   - *Name of an airport*
   - *Name of a bus station*
   - *Name of a train station*

4. *Day of arrival*

5. *Date of arrival*

6. *Time of arrival (include a.m. or p.m.)*

7. Your *telephone number, name, and address*

Telegram form courtesy of Western Union Telegraph Co.

Vacation Postcards

You can send picture postcards to friends when you go on vacation or when you want to keep in touch.

1 WITH YOUR CLASS: Vocabulary
Read this postcard with your class, and add more words to the vocabulary list.

2 WRITE YOUR OWN: Postcard to Your English Class
Complete this postcard. Address it to your English class.

Hi!
    Having a wonderful time in _____ (2) . I'm enjoying the _____ (3) . The weather is _____ (4) .
_____ (5) .
_____ (6)

(1)

(7)

CHAPTER FOLLOW-UP

1 Draw a map showing how to get from your home to the post office.

2 Get a driver's license application from your state. What kind of information is the same as the Massachusetts application? What is different? Fill out the application.

3 What do tourists usually buy as souvenirs in your native country? Write a list on the board of souvenirs they buy.

4 What do people in your native country want from the U.S.A.? Write a list on the board of things they want.

5 Write a list of things you would pack if you were going on a trip to your favorite place. Then write your list on the board and explain it to the class.

6 Write a friendly letter thanking your partner for the visit you had (see **Friendly Letter About a Visit**).

7 What is a traveler's check? What are the advantages of using them? Have you ever used them? If not, why not?

8 Skim the chapter and circle the new vocabulary words. Then make a list of the words you remember (examples: *landmark, vehicle, urgent, declaration*).

Employment

Teacher's Notes

Student Objectives:
- *To become acquainted with forms related to employment (Social Security, job applications, Federal Income Tax, and Unemployment)*
- *To write a résumé.*

Sequence

1 Tell the students not to fill in the blanks until the class has discussed the page.

2 The forms in this chapter are very complicated and include an intimidating amount of specialized vocabulary. Find out which forms your students need to use and concentrate on those forms.

3 Read the introductory information at the top of each page with the students.

4 Read through each form with the students, making sure they understand the vocabulary. Fill in the forms together, step by step. Take your time.

5 Complete the pages titled **Résumé, Responding to a Help Wanted Ad,** and **Employment Application** as a unit.

6 A résumé prepared in advance is especially useful for job applicants with limited English, even though it is difficult to compose. Discuss with the class the ways the students can use their résumé to help them fill out an employment application and to prepare for an employment interview.

Résumé

When you apply for a job, always take a copy of your *résumé* (a summary of your educational background and work experience). The résumé will make it easier for you to fill out the employment application. You can also give it to the person who interviews you for a job.

1 WITH YOUR CLASS: Sample Résumé

Look at this sample résumé with your class. Use it as a guide to help you fill in your résumé on the next page. Notice that you must begin with your most recent education and work experience.

```
                         José E. Martínez
                         2914 Jerome Ave.
                      Bronx, New York  10468
                         (212) 365-8758

Education:

    1978              A.A., North Central Community College, Brooklyn,
                      New York
    1975              High School Equivalency Diploma (GED), Commun-
                      ity Center, New York, New York

Work Experience:

    1976-present:     International Shoe Machinery Co., Yonkers,
                      New York.  Foreman.  Responsible for 8 workers
                      in supply department, stocktaking, ordering
                      supplies, distributing supplies to various
                      departments.

    1974-1976:        Union Shoe Factory, Albany, New York
                      Team Leader, stitching department.  Promoted
                      from stitcher.

    1973-1974:        United Trucking Co., Princeton, New Jersey
                      Truckdriver.  Responsible for maintenance of
                      truck, delivering cargo to companies in east-
                      ern states.

Skills:               Organizing and supervising inventory control.
                      Operating and maintaining stitching equipment.
                      Driving and maintaining Mack truck (piggy back).
                      Bilingual in Spanish and English

References:           Mr. Edward Sweeny
                      International Shoe Machinery Co.
                      1660 Third Avenue
                      Yonkers, New York

                      Rev. John Kendall
                      246 Flower Ave.
                      Peekskill, New York
```

2 WRITE YOUR OWN: Your Résumé

Fill in this résumé for yourself. Then type it on a piece of 8½" × 11" white paper. Do not copy the italicized words.

_____

(your name)

_____

(your street address)

_____

(your city, state, zip code)

_____

(your area code and telephone number)

EDUCATION:

| *(year)* | *(degree)* | *(name of school)* | *(location)* |

_____

_____

EXPERIENCE:

_____:

(from)   *(to)*   *(name of company)*   *(location)*

_____

(job responsibilities)

_____:

_____

_____:

_____

SKILLS: _____

_____

_____

REFERENCES: _____

(name)   *(name)*

_____

(title)   *(title)*

_____

(address)   *(address)*

_____

Responding to a Help Wanted Ad

Some job advertisements in the help wanted section of the newspaper give phone numbers to call. Other ads direct you to send in your résumé. When you send your résumé, include a cover letter.

1 WITH YOUR CLASS: Help Wanted Ads

Read these help wanted ads with your class and choose a job you want to apply for. Then fill in the cover letter on the next page to send in with your résumé.

Help Wanted

NURSES AIDES
Full or part time
For modern nursing home
Excellent fringe benefits
Call Mrs. Donovan, R.N.
532-0768

FULL CHARGE BOOKKEEPER
Full-time position requiring typing.
Call 927-5000
or apply in person
**NORTHERN
SHOE BINDINGS CO., INC.**
L-Building, Balch St.,
Beverly, MA 01915

SECRETARY
Good typing and general office skills. Pleasant telephone manner. Shorthand a plus. Contact: Mr. Timothy for appointment
532-1116

ARE YOU GREAT?
$225-$250
Secretary to sales mgr. If you have excellent typing and shorthand with ability to take charge, then this exciting position could be yours.
**SNELLING & SNELLING
EMPLOYMENT CONSULTANTS**
30 STATE STREET, LYNN 599-9200

SWITCHBOARD OPERATOR/ TYPIST
35/40 wpm. Excellent telephone skills. Will train right person. Excellent fringes including education assistance program. For personal interview call or write.
UNITED TECHNOLOGIES
Essex Group
247 Lynnfield St.
Peabody, MA 01960
531-7100 Ext. 31
An equal opportunity employer
M/F/H/V

Help Wanted

WORD PROCESSING OPEN
Opportunities at all levels for W.P. Specialists with experience. Tuition reimbursement.
MICKEE'S PLACEMENT SERVICE
462 Broadway
At Route 1 Lynnfield
581-0623

MANAGER FOR HEALTH SPA
Woman's World Health Spa in Danvers is seeking experienced manager with strong sales background. Responsible for management of staff, exercise, diet, promotional activities and sales. Salary plus commission. Good opportunity for a motivated person.
Call between 3 and 7 p.m.
774-0223

LABORERS
$7.64
per hour plus benefits
One full-time and part-time employee. For all phases for building and ground maintenance.
Send resumes to Peabody Housing Authority 75-81 Central St., Peabody, MA 01960. Last day of filing February 13, 1981
Affirmative Action/Equal Opportunity Employer

PROPERTY MANAGER
Maintenance oriented, for large multi tenant industrial properties in Salem and Andover, Mass. Good salary and benefits; Steady full-time job.
Call Bruce Erikson
289-2506 or 744-0556
or send resume to
SHETLAND PROPERTIES
P.O. Box 986
Salem, MA 01970

Help Wanted

R.N. or L.P.N.
Full or part time, for modern nursing home. Excellent fringe benefits.
Call Mrs. Donovan
532-0768

HOUSEKEEPER
Mature person. 7 a.m. to 2 p.m. Several days per week.
LAFAYETTE CONVALESCENT HOME
631-4535
Call Mrs. Edwards
between 8 a.m. and 2 p.m.

NURSES' AIDES
Positions currently available, part time, 11:15-7:15. Weekends, 7-3:30. Formal nurse's aide training program. Excellent salary and benefit program. Apply in person for interview between 10 a.m. & 4 p.m.
LIBERTY PAVILION NURSING HOME
56 Liberty Street
Danvers
an equal opportunity employer

FOREMAN FOR LATHE DEPT.
Must be familiar with tape controlled machines and conventional type. Will supervise small group of people. Top salary for right person. Right person does not need supervisory experience but does need good machine shop knowledge.

QUALITY CONTROL INSPECTOR
To supervise and manage small group of people. Must have experience in setting up proper quality control procedures. Top salary for capable person. All replies held in strict confidence.
Reply to:
P.O. Box C.D. 1048
Salem, MA 01970

Help Wanted

Work at home on the phone servicing our customers in your spare time. Over 18. 777-3205.

DIETARY UTILITY PERSON
Mature person. 2 p.m. to 7 p.m. shift. Monday through Friday. Will require some supervising. Call for appointment, 631-4535. Lafayette Convalescent Home.

RELIEF COOK
Part time position available for a reliable person to prepare meals for 100 bed extended care facility. Willing to train responsible cook in preparation and service of therapeutic diets. Excellent salary.
For further info call:
Ms. Aschiero, Administrator at 774-6955.
CEDAR GLEN
Skilled Nursing Facility

Registered Medical Technologist
Part Time
For Chemistry Lab.
7 a.m. to 12 noon,
Monday thru Friday.
Contact Mr. Dow at:
531-2900, ext. 256.
J.B. Thomas Hospital
15 King Street
Peabody, MA 01960

Classified advertisements courtesy of *The Salem News*, Salem, Mass.

2 WRITE YOUR OWN: A Cover Letter

Prepare a cover letter to send with your résumé. Type the résumé and the letter if possible.

```
                                        _____
                                                (1)
                                        _____
                                                (1)
                                        _____
                                                (2)


        _____
                (3)
        _____
                (4)
        _____
                (4)
Dear _____ :
                (5)
        Enclosed is my résumé.  I would like to
apply for the job of _____ .
                                (6)
I hope to have the opportunity to discuss
this position with you at an interview.


                        Sincerely,


                        _____
                                (7)
```

1. *Your address*
2. *The date*
3. *Name of the person to whom you are writing (if listed in the ad)*
4. *Name and address of the company*
5. *Choose one:*
   - Sir
   - Madam
   - Personnel Director
   - *Name of person listed in ad*
6. *Name of job*
7. *Your signature*

Employment Application

Many employers have application forms to fill out when you apply for work. Every company has a different application form. Most applications ask about your past employment, education, United States military service, and preferred work. This information from your résumé will help you to fill out this sample application.

1 WRITE YOUR OWN: Employment Application

Fill out this application. Use the information from your resume.

EMPLOYMENT APPLICATION

PERSONAL

NAME: _____ SOCIAL SECURITY NO. _____

PRESENT ADDRESS: _____ TELEPHONE NUMBER _____

(NUMBER)   (STREET)

(CITY)   (STATE)   (ZIP CODE)

EDUCATIONAL

NAMES OF SCHOOLS	CITY & STATE	MONTH & YEAR From:	To:	Graduated Yes ☐ No ☐		YEAR	DEGREE
				☐	☐		
				☐	☐		
				☐	☐		
				☐	☐		

WORK EXPERIENCE & MILITARY

Previous work experience and service in the U.S. Armed Forces. Account completely for the last five years.

NAME & ADDRESS OF LAST EMPLOYER	DATES	KIND OF BUSINESS	DUTIES	APPROX. WEEKLY SALARY	REASON FOR LEAVING
1	FROM: 19				
	TO: 19				
2	FROM: 19				
	TO: 19				
3	FROM: 19				
	TO: 19				
4	FROM: 19				
	TO: 19				

EMPLOYMENT DESIRED:

☐ Permanent   ☐ Temporary   ☐ Part-time   ☐ Summer

WORK PREFERRED _____

WHO SHOULD BE NOTIFIED IN CASE OF EMERGENCY?

NAME: _____   TELEPHONE NO. _____

PLEASE READ BEFORE SIGNING:

I affirm that all information included on this application is true and correct. Any false information I have given can be considered sufficient cause for discharge. I authorize all former employers to answer questions in reference to this application.   Signature _____   Date _____

Employee's Withholding Allowance Certificate (W-4)

When you start a new job, your employer gives you an Employee's Withholding Allowance Certificate (Form W-4) to fill out. This form shows your employer how many allowances you claim on your federal income tax.

1 WITH YOUR CLASS: Reading a W-4

Read this W-4 form with your class and discuss the vocabulary.

Form **W-4**
(Rev. May 1977)

Department of the Treasury
Internal Revenue Service

Employee's Withholding Allowance Certificate
(Use for Wages Paid After May 31, 1977)

This certificate is for income tax withholding purposes only. It will remain in effect until you change it. If you claim exemption from withholding, you will have to file a new certificate on or before April 30 of next year.

Type or print your full name

Your social security number

Home address (number and street or rural route)

City or town, State, and ZIP code

Marital Status

☐ Single ☐ Married
☐ Married, but withhold at higher Single rate

Note: If married, but legally separated, or spouse is a nonresident alien, check the single block.

1 Total number of allowances you are claiming . . . .

2 Additional amount, if any, you want deducted from each pay (if your employer agrees) . . . . $

3 I claim exemption from withholding (see instructions). Enter "Exempt" . . . .

Under the penalties of perjury, I certify that the number of withholding exemptions and allowances claimed on this certificate does not exceed the number to which I am entitled. If claiming exemption from withholding, I certify that I incurred no liability for Federal income tax for last year and that I anticipate that I will incur no liability for Federal income tax for this year.

Signature ▶ --- Date ▶ ---------------------------------------, 19 ---------

---

2 WITH YOUR CLASS: Filling Out a W-4

a. Fill out the top part of the form. Print your name, address, Social Security number, and marital status.

b. Look at 1: *Total number of allowances you are claiming.* Claim one allowance for every person you support, including yourself. Write the number in the box at the right.

c. Look at 2: *Additional amount, if any, you want deducted from each paycheck (if your employer agrees).* If you know you will have to pay extra tax to the U.S. Government, you may want your employer to take out extra money from your pay. Most people write 0 in this space because they do not want extra money deducted from their pay.

d. Look at 3: *I claim exemption from withholding.* If you are single and will earn less than $2,200 this year and didn't have to pay income tax last year, write *exempt.* If you are married and will earn less than $3,200 this year and didn't have to pay income tax last year, write *exempt.* (Or if you didn't earn enough money to pay income tax last year and you think you won't earn enough money to pay income tax this year, write *exempt.*)

e. Read the fine print.

f. Sign the form and write the date.

Social Security—Request for Statement of Earnings

If you want to know how much money you have earned in the Social Security system, fill in a card like this at your Social Security office. Then mail it to the Social Security Administration.

1 WITH YOUR CLASS: Request for Statement of Earnings

Fill out this Request for Statement of Earnings. Follow the directions on the front of the card.

YOUR SOCIAL SECURITY EARNINGS RECORD

For a *free* statement of earnings credited to your social security record, complete other side of this card. Use card for only *one* person.

All covered wages and self-employment income are reported under your *name* and social security *number*. So show your name and number *exactly* as on your card. If you ever used another name or number, show this too.

Be sure to put a stamp on this card or it won't be delivered. You can mail the card in a stamped envelope if you wish.

If you have a separate question about social security, or want to discuss your statement when you get it, the people at any social security office will be glad to help you.

Form SSA-7004 PC (1-79)
(Prior Editions May Be Used Until Supply Is Exhausted)

POSTAGE REQUIRED

SOCIAL SECURITY ADMINISTRATION
P. O. BOX 57
BALTIMORE, MARYLAND 21203

(Please read instructions on back before completing)

REQUEST FOR SOCIAL SECURITY STATEMENT OF EARNINGS

Your social security number

Date of Birth

Month	Day	Year

Print Name and Address in ink or use typewriter

Please send a statement of my social security earnings to:

Name _____

Number & Street _____

City & State _____ Zip Code _____

Sign Your Name Here _____
(Do Not Print)

I am the individual to whom the record pertains. I understand that if I knowingly and willingly request or receive a record about an individual under false pretenses I would be guilty of a Federal crime and could be fined up to $5,000.

If you ever used a name (such as a maiden name) on a social security card different from the one above, please print name here:

Filling Out an Income Tax Return

On April 15 every year, people who earned money in the United States during the previous year must file an income tax return with the United States Internal Revenue Service (IRS). Form 1040A is the *short form*. Many people get help in completing their income tax forms.

1 ON THE BOARD: Income Tax Assistance

In your community, where can you get help in completing your income tax forms? Is the assistance free? Do you have to pay a fee? Make a list on the board of places you can go for help.

2 WRITE YOUR OWN: 1040A (Top Half)

The top half of the 1040A asks for personal information. Fill it in for yourself.

a. Fill in your name, address, Social Security number, and occupation at the top of the form.

b. Check *yes* or *no* for the Presidential Election Campaign Fund. ☐

c. Filing Status: Write a check ☐ in one of the four boxes.

d. Exemptions #5a–5d: Fill in all the information on the left. Transfer the information to the three boxes on the right. In the fourth box, write the total number of exemptions claimed.

Form 1040A Department of the Treasury—Internal Revenue Service
U.S. Individual Income Tax Return 1980

Use IRS label. Otherwise, please print or type.	Your first name and initial (if joint return, also give spouse's name and initial)	Last name	Your social security number
	Present home address (Number and street, including apartment number, or rural route)		Spouse's social security no.
	City, town or post office, State and ZIP code	Your occupation ▶	
		Spouse's occupation ▶	

Presidential Election Campaign Fund ▶ Do you want $1 to go to this fund? . . . . ☐ Yes ☐ No

If joint return, does your spouse want $1 to go to this fund? . . . ☐ Yes ☐ No

Note: *Checking "Yes" will not increase your tax or reduce your refund.*

Requested by Census Bureau for Revenue Sharing ▶

A Where do you live (actual location of residence)? (See page 6 of Instructions.) State / City, village, borough, etc.

B Do you live within the legal limits of a city, village, etc.? ☐ Yes ☐ No

C In what county do you live?

D In what township do you live?

For Privacy Act Notice, see page 27 of Instructions

For IRS use only

Filing Status
Check Only One Box.

1 ☐ Single
2 ☐ Married filing joint return (even if only one had income)
3 ☐ Married filing separate return. Enter spouse's social security no. above and full name here ▶
4 ☐ Head of household. (See pages 7 and 8 of Instructions.) If qualifying person is your unmarried child, enter child's name ▶

Exemptions
Always check the box labeled Yourself. Check other boxes if they apply.

5a ☐ Yourself   ☐ 65 or over   ☐ Blind
b ☐ Spouse   ☐ 65 or over   ☐ Blind

} Enter number of boxes checked on 5a and b ▶ ☐

c First names of your dependent children who lived with you ▶ ....

} Enter number of children listed on 5c ▶ ☐

d Other dependents:

(1) Name	(2) Relationship	(3) Number of months lived in your home.	(4) Did dependent have income of $1,000 or more?	(5) Did you provide more than one-half of dependent's support?

Enter number of other dependents ▶ ☐

6 Total number of exemptions claimed . . . .

Add numbers entered in boxes above ▶ ☐

W–2 Here

140

3 WITH YOUR CLASS: 1040A (Bottom Half)

The bottom half of the 1040A asks for financial information. With your class, use the instructions below to fill in the bottom half of the form.

a. Imagine that your wages and salaries amounted to $12,158.00. Write this amount in box 7.

b. Imagine that your interest income was $210.00. Write this amount in box 8.

c. Imagine that you had no dividends or exclusions. Write a dash (—) in boxes 9a, 9b, and 9c.

d. Imagine that you had no unemployment compensation. Write a dash (—) in box 10b.

e. Add $12,158.00 and $210.00 to find your adjusted gross income. Write the total in box 11.

f. Imagine that you did not contribute to candidates for public office. Write a dash in box 12a.

g. Imagine that you want IRS to figure your tax. Do not write anything in boxes 12b, 12c, 13, 14a, 14b, 15, 16, or 17.

Please Sign Here: Imagine that you filled out your form with no help. Write your signature. Above the date, write **April 14, 19____** (this year).

Please Attach Copy B of Forms

7 Wages, salaries, tips, etc. *(Attach Forms W–2. See page 10 of Instructions)* 7

8 Interest income *(See pages 3 and 10 of Instructions)* 8

9a Dividends ______ *(See pages 3 and 10 of Instructions)* 9b Exclusion ______ Subtract line 9b from 9a 9c

10a Unemployment compensation (insurance). Total received from Form(s) 1099–UC ______

b Taxable amount, if any, from worksheet on page 10 of Instructions 10b

11 Adjusted gross income *(add lines 7, 8, 9c, and 10b). If under $10,000, see page 12 of Instructions on "Earned Income Credit"* 11

12a Credit for contributions to candidates for public office. *(See page 11 of Instructions)* 12a

IF YOU WANT IRS TO FIGURE YOUR TAX, PLEASE STOP HERE AND SIGN BELOW.

Attach Payment Here

b Total Federal income tax withheld *(If line 7 is more than $25,900, see page 11 of Instructions)* 12b

c Earned income credit *(from page 12 of Instructions)* . . . 12c

13 Total *(add lines 12a, b, and c)* 13

14a Tax on the amount on line 11. *(See page 13 of Instructions; then find your tax in the Tax Tables on pages 15–26)* 14a

b Advance earned income credit (EIC) *(from Form W–2)* . . . 14b

15 Total *(add lines 14a and 14b)* 15

16 If line 13 is larger than line 15, enter amount to be **REFUNDED TO YOU** . . . . ▶ 16

17 If line 15 is larger than line 13, enter **BALANCE DUE.** Attach check or money order for full amount payable to "Internal Revenue Service." Write your social security number on check or money order . ▶ 17

Please Sign Here

Under penalties of perjury, I declare that I have examined this return, including accompanying schedules and statements, and to the best of my knowledge and belief, it is true, correct, and complete. Declaration of preparer (other than taxpayer) is based on all information of which preparer has any knowledge.

▶ Your signature Date ▶ Spouse's signature (if filing jointly, BOTH must sign even if only one had income)

Paid Preparer's Use Only

Preparer's signature and date ▶ Check if self-employed ▶ ☐ Preparer's social security no.

Firm's name (or yours, if self-employed) and address ▶ E.I. No. ▶ ZIP code ▶

★ U.S. Government Printing Office: 1980-0-313-446 E.I. #52-1074467

Form **1040A** (1980)

Unemployment

If you lose your job, you are very often entitled to unemployment compensation. Each state decides how much to pay, requirements for eligibility, and the length of eligibility.

1 WITH YOUR CLASS: Your Local Unemployment Office

Where is your local unemployment office? What is its official name? Look it up in the telephone directory under the name of your state and write the address and the telephone number here:

_____   _____

address   telephone number

2 WITH YOUR CLASS: Filling Out a Weekly Benefit Statement

In some states, you must fill out a statement every week when you pick up your unemployment check. This is a statement from Massachusetts. Fill it out. Does the statement from your state look the same?

COMMONWEALTH OF MASSACHUSETTS • DIVISION OF EMPLOYMENT SECURITY   Social Security Account Number

J job insurance   ☐☐☐-☐☐-☐☐☐☐

WEEKLY BENEFIT STATEMENT   B Y E   DO NOT WRITE IN THIS BLOCK

WARNING: ANSWER ALL QUESTIONS CAREFULLY. CLAIMS ARE INVESTIGATED. FALSE STATEMENTS CAN BRING A FINE OR JAIL OR BOTH.

1. **DURING THE WEEK ENDING**_____
   a. Did you work either for an employer or in self-employment? . . . .   YES ☐   NO ☐
      If "YES", enter earnings $_____ Name of employer _____
   b. Did you look for work with anyone other than your last employer? . . . .   YES ☐   NO ☐
   c. Did you refuse any work? . . . .   YES ☐   NO ☐
   d. Did you attend any school or college? . . . .   YES ☐   NO ☐
   e. Did you receive, or have you applied for, any money for reasons below? . . . . .   YES ☐   NO ☐
      (1) Severance, dismissal or retroactive pay (3) Bonus or Gratuity (5) Pension of Any Kind
      (2) Vacation pay (4) Workman's Compensation (6) Education or training allowance as a veteran
   f. Were you able and willing to accept work on all **full time** shifts, customary for
      your occupation . . . .   YES ☐   NO ☐
   g. Did the number of your dependent children increase or decrease? . . . .   YES ☐   NO ☐
2. **DID YOU CHANGE ADDRESS SINCE YOU LAST REPORTED?** . . . .   YES ☐   NO ☐
   If "YES", enter new address_____

☐☐☐☐☐
Zip Code

The above answers are given under the penalties of perjury.

Signature _____

IMPORTANT! (See Over)

Form 3099 Rev. 1-80 3000M-5-80-152729

CHAPTER FOLLOW-UP

1   How can you use your résumé in an employment interview?

2   What kinds of jobs are being advertised now in your local newspaper? Look in the Help Wanted section.

3   Where can you use a Social Security card? What is Social Security?

4   Look at the stub from your paycheck. Can you find the amount withheld for Social Security? It is listed under F.I.C.A. (Federal Insurance Contribution Act).

5   What is unemployment compensation? Do people receive unemployment compensation in your native country?

6   When do you have to fill out a W-4 form? How many exemptions would you claim?

Notes

Teacher's Notes

Student Objectives:
- *to learn to write various kinds of notes*
- *to become familiar with writing signs and notices in the United States.*

Sequence

1   Tell the students not to fill in the blanks until the class has discussed the page.

2   To introduce each page with a note, provide a model of the note by reading the note to the students, using the vocabulary from the list. To introduce the other pages, look over the illustrations with the students.

3   Discuss the meaning and uses of the note or the illustration.

4   Ask the students for suggestions for other vocabulary. Write the vocabulary words on the board and discuss them. Have the students copy the words in their books.

5   Fill in the note on the page. Be sure the choices fit together (for example, in the exercise at the top of the opposite page, you cannot *borrow . . . . a ride home.*

6   Do the other exercises on the page.

Short Notes—Requests and Offers

1 WITH YOUR CLASS: Vocabulary
Read these notes. Add more words to the vocabulary lists.

2 WITH YOUR PARTNER: Note to Ask for Something
Write this short note to your partner.

_____)
(1)

May I _____
(2)

_____ ?
(3)

_____
(4)

1. *Your partner's name*
2. *Choose one:*
   • borrow
   • have
3. *Choose one:*
   • a ride home
   • your pen
   • a piece of paper
   • your homework
4. *Your signature*

3 WITH YOUR PARTNER: Note to Offer Something
Write this short note to your partner.

_____)
(1)

Would you like _____

_____
(2)

_____ ?
(3)

_____
(4)

1. *Your partner's name*
2. *Choose one:*
   • to go for coffee
   • to study together
   • a ride home
   • *other:* _____
   _____
3. *Choose one:*
   • after class
   • tonight
   • *other:* _____
   _____
   _____
4. *Your signature*

Notes for a Notice Board

1 WITH YOUR CLASS: Notices

Look at the categories on this notice board. Read the notes in each category. What are they about?

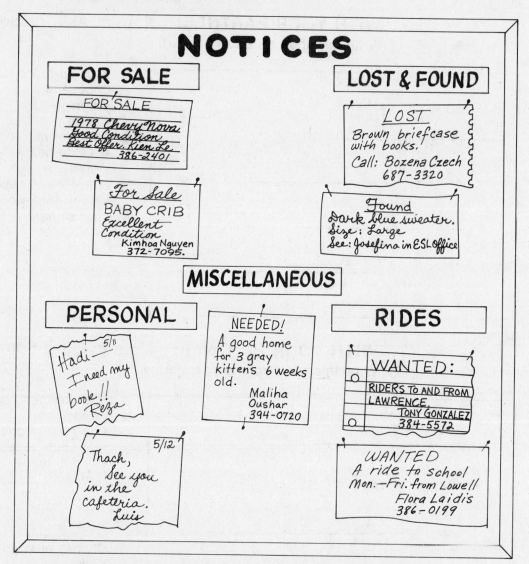

2 WITH YOUR CLASS: Class Notice Board

Does your class or school have a notice board? Look at the notes on it. What are they about? If your class does not have a notice board, make one. Use it for messages and announcements to other members of the class.

3 WRITE YOUR OWN: Note for a Notice Board

Write a note for your class notice board.

Making Signs

1 WITH A PARTNER: Signs

Read the situations with a partner. Decide which signs are appropriate.
Print them under each situation.

Situations:

1. You need to sell your car.

   _____

2. The toilet is leaking and it gets worse every time someone flushes it.

   _____

3. The coffee machine at school does not work.

   _____

4. There is a vacant apartment in the building where you are the superintendent.

   _____

5. A classmate is returning to class after being sick for a month.

   _____

6. Smoking is not allowed in this area.

   _____

2 WITH YOUR CLASS: Signs for Your Classroom

Does your classroom need a sign? Is there a special reference area? a coffee area? a smoking area? Discuss as a class the possible signs you can make. Print them and hang them up.

Note to Arrange a Conference

Sometimes you may write a note to ask for a conference with a counselor, work supervisor, or with your child's teacher.

1   WITH YOUR CLASS: Vocabulary
Read this note with your class and add more words to the vocabulary list.

2   WRITE YOUR OWN: Note to Arrange an Appointment
Complete this note to arrange an appointment.

_____
(1)

Dear _____,
(2)
I would like to meet with you to discuss _____
(3)
_____.
I can come in any _____
(4)
_____.
Sincerely,

_____
(5)

1. *Date*
2. *Name of supervisor, counselor or teacher.*
3. *Choose one:*
   • a problem
   • my future plans
   • a personal matter
   • my daughter (name)'s schoolwork
   • my son (name)'s schoolwork
   • *other:* _____

   _____

4. *Choose one:*
   • Monday
   • afternoon
   • *other:* _____

   _____

5. *Your signature*

3   WRITE YOUR OWN: Note to Your Teacher
Write a note to your English teacher to request a conference.

Early Dismissal Note

If your child must leave school before regular dismissal time, write a note to the teacher.

1 WITH YOUR CLASS: Vocabulary

Read this note with your class and add more words to the vocabulary list.

2 WRITE YOUR OWN: Note for Early Dismissal from School

Complete this note.

Dear _____ ,
Please dismiss _____
at _____ *today*
because of _____ .
        Sincerely,
_____

1. *Date*
2. *Your child's teacher's name*
3. *Your child's name*
4. *Choose one:*
   - 10:30 a.m.
   - 2:00 p.m.
   - 12:00 noon
5. *Choose one:*
   - an appointment
   - an obligation
   - *other:* a _____

     an _____
6. *Your signature*

3 WITH YOUR PARTNER: Early Dismissal Note

Imagine your partner is your child. Write a note to the teacher to tell why your partner must leave school early.

Note of Apology

1 **WITH YOUR CLASS:** Vocabulary

Read this note with your class and add more words to the vocabulary list.

2 **WRITE YOUR OWN:** Note of Apology

Complete this note.

_____ (1)

Dear _____ , (2)

Sorry I _____ (3)

_____

_____ . I had (4)

_____ . (5)

I hope we can get together soon.

_____ (6)

1. *Today's date*
2. *Name of person you are apologizing to*
3. *Choose one:*
   - missed seeing you
   - missed our appointment
   - missed the party
   - forgot your birthday
   - other: _____
   _____
4. *Choose one:*
   - yesterday
   - last Saturday
   - today
   - other: _____
   _____
5. *Choose one:*
   - to work overtime
   - a headache
   - to leave early
   - too many things on my mind
   - other: _____
   _____
6. *Your signature*

Permission Slips

Children bring home permission slips from school before their class goes on a trip. Parents sign the slips to allow their children to go on the trip. Permission slips are usually mimeographed. Often the school also sends home a note asking for parents to go on the trip as chaperones for the children.

1 WRITE YOUR OWN: Filling in a Permission Slip

Fill in the blanks.

1. *Your child's name*
2. *Your signature*

To the teacher:

_____ has my permission to go the Science
(1)
Museum on Friday, March 27.

_____
(parent's signature)
(2)

2 WITH YOUR PARTNER: Permission Note

Pretend that your partner is your child. Your child's class is planning a trip to the zoo next Thursday. Your child lost the permission slip. Write a permission note for your child. Use the vocabulary from the permission slip above.

Absence and Late Notes

When your child is late to school or is returning to school after being absent, you write a note to the teacher. The note explains when and why your child was not in school.

1 WITH YOUR CLASS: Vocabulary

Read this note with your class. Add more words to the vocabulary list.

2 WRITE YOUR OWN: Note for Absence or Lateness

Complete the note.

Dear _____ (1)

Dear _____ (2) ,

_____ (3) *was*

_____ (4) _____ (5)

because of _____ (6)

_____ .

Sincerely,

_____ (7)

1. *Today's date*
2. *The teacher's name*
3. *Your child's name*
4. *Choose one:*
   - absent
   - late
5. *Choose one:*
   - yesterday
   - this morning
   - Friday
   - last week
   - *other:* _____

   _____

   _____
6. *Choose one:*
   - family obligations
   - a death in the family
   - an appointment with the doctor
   - *other:* _____

   _____

   _____
7. *Your signature*

3 WITH YOUR PARTNER: Absence Note

Pretend that your partner is your sick child. Write an absence note to your teacher for your partner.

4 WITH YOUR CLASS: Customs in Other Countries

Are absence notes required in your native country? Tell the class.

5 WRITE YOUR OWN: Late Note

Pretend that you were late to class today. Write a note to your teacher to explain why you were late. (This late note is for practice. Adults usually do not need late notes.)

Cancellation and Postponement Notices

Sometimes it is necessary to cancel or postpone a meeting or an event because of bad weather or an emergency. Local radio stations announce cancellations and postponements as a public service. How does your school notify students of cancellations or postponements?

1 WITH YOUR CLASS: Vocabulary

Read this notice with your class. Add more words to the vocabulary list.

2 WRITE YOUR OWN: Notice for Cancellation or Postponement

Complete this notice.

_____
(1)

The _____
_____ *that was*
scheduled for today at
(2)
_____
has been _____
(3)
_____ .
(4)

1. *Today's date*
2. *Choose one:*
   - Alcoholics Anonymous meeting
   - Chamber of Commerce awards dinner
   - Spring Flower Festival
   - *other:* _____
   _____

3. *Choose one:*
   - the city auditorium
   - the public library
   - *other:* _____
   _____

4. *Choose one:*
   - cancelled
   - postponed until further notice
   - postponed to next Thursday
   - *other:* _____
   _____
   _____

3 WITH YOUR CLASS: Class Cancellation Notice

Imagine the teacher is sick. Write a cancellation notice for your class on the board.

4 WRITE YOUR OWN: Postponement Notice

Imagine that your teacher scheduled a film for tomorrow at the library. The film is postponed until next Monday. Write a postponement notice.

155

Notes for Housing Complaints

If something is unsatisfactory in your apartment or building, write a *complaint note* to the superintendent, landlord, or landlady.

1   WITH YOUR CLASS: Vocabulary

Read this note with your class and add more words to the vocabulary list.

2   WRITE YOUR OWN: Housing Complaint Note

Complete the note.

_____
(1)

Dear _____ ,
(2)

Please do something

about _____
(3)

_____ .
(4)

I have had this problem

_____ .
(5)

_____
(6)

1. *Date*
2. *Name of superintendent, landlord or landlady*
3. *Choose one:*
   - the sink
   - the heat
   - the kitchen faucet
   - the stopped-up toilet
   - the broken window
   - the cockroaches
   - *other:* _____

   _____

   _____

4. *Choose one:*
   - right away
   - as soon as possible
   - immediately
   - today
   - at once
   - *other:* _____

   _____

   _____

5. *Choose one:*
   - since last week
   - for a week
   - since April
   - for a month
   - *other:* _____

   _____

6. *Your signature*

3   WITH A PARTNER: Complaint Note

Pretend your partner is your superintendent, landlord, or landlady. Write a complaint note to your partner. Use the vocabulary above.

Thank-You Notes:
Thank You for Remembering

1   WITH YOUR CLASS: Vocabulary
Read this note with your class and add more words to the vocabulary list.

2   WRITE YOUR OWN: Thank-You Note
Complete this note.

_____ (1)

Dear _____ , (2)

_____ for (3)

remembering me _____

_____ I (4)

really _____ (5)

the _____ . (6)

_____) (7)

_____ (8)

1. *Date*
2. *Name of a relative or friend*
3. *Choose one:*
   - Thanks
   - Thank you
4. *Choose one:*
   - on my graduation
   - on my birthday
   - when I was ill
   - *other:* _____
   _____
5. *Choose one:*
   - appreciated
   - liked
   - loved
   - *other:* _____
   _____
6. *Choose one:*
   - card
   - gift
   - flowers
   - *other:* _____
   _____
7. *Choose one:*
   - Love
   - Fondly
   - Your friend
   - *other:* _____
8. *Your signature*

3   ON THE BOARD: Saying Thank You in Your Native Language
How do you say "thank you" in your native language? Write the word(s) on the board and teach the class the pronunciation.

Thank-You Notes:
Thank You for a Gift

1 WITH YOUR CLASS: Thank-You Note
Read this note with your class. Add more words to the vocabulary list.

2 WRITE YOUR OWN: Thank-You Note
Complete this note.

Dear _____ (2)
Thanks so much for
the _____ (3). It's
_____ (4)
_____ (5))
_____ (6)

_____ (1)

1. *Date*
2. *Name of a relative or friend*
3. *Choose one:*
   - record
   - scarf
   - book
   - *other:* _____
   _____
   _____
4. *Choose one:*
   - beautiful
   - very special
   - exactly what I needed
   - *other:* _____
   _____
   _____
5. *Choose one:*
   - Love
   - Sincerely
   - Fondly
   - *other:* _____
   _____
   _____
6. *Your signature*

3 WITH YOUR CLASS: Thank-You Note for a Gift
Write the name of a nice gift on a small piece of paper. Fold up the paper and put all the students' papers in a pile. Pick a paper from the pile. Write a thank-you note for the gift on the paper.

4 WITH A PARTNER: Thank-You Note
Pretend that your partner gave you a Christmas gift. Write a thank-you note for the gift.

Thank-You Notes:
Thank You for a Visit

1 WITH YOUR CLASS: Vocabulary

Read this note with your class. Add more words to the vocabulary list.

2 WRITE YOUR OWN: Thank-You Note

Complete this note.

A _____ (1)

Dear _____ (2) ,

_____ (3)

was a real pleasure. Thank

you for _____ (4) .

I _____ (5) .

_____ (6) ,

_____ (7)

1. *Date*
2. *Name of a friend*
3. *Choose one:*
   - My visit with you
   - Last weekend
   - Visiting you
   - *other:* _____
   - _____
4. *Choose one:*
   - everything
   - putting me up
   - your hospitality
   - *other:* _____
   - _____
5. *Choose one:*
   - had a wonderful time
   - enjoyed every moment
   - *other:* _____
   - _____
6. *Choose one:*
   - Love
   - Sincerely
   - *other:* _____
   - _____
7. *Your signature*

3 WRITE YOUR OWN: Longer Thank-You Note

Write a longer thank-you note for a real visit. Include in line 5 something specific that you enjoyed during your visit.

Thank-You Notes:
Thank You for Your Help

1 WITH YOUR CLASS: Vocabulary
Read this note with your class. Add more words to the vocabulary list.

2 WRITE YOUR OWN: Thank-You Note
Complete this note in appreciation of assistance.

_____ (1)

Dear _____ (2),
I want to thank you
for _____ (3). I
really appreciate your taking
the time _____ (4)
_____,
_____ (5),
_____ (6)

1. *Date*
2. *Name of the person who helped you*
3. *Choose one:*
   • helping me
   • all the help you've given me
4. *Choose one:*
   • to see me
   • to talk with me
   • to do so much for me
   • *other:* _____
   _____
   _____
5. *Choose one:*
   • Sincerely
   • Sincerely yours
   • *other:* _____
   _____
   _____
6. *Your signature*

3 WRITE YOUR OWN: Your Thank-You Note
Write a thank-you note to someone who has really helped you.

CHAPTER FOLLOW-UP

1 When would you write a short note in English? (Examples: to borrow a pen, to say thank you for a gift). Make a list of these occasions on the board.

2 Look back at the supermarket shopping list in Chapter 5. Discuss the differences you see between a list and a note.

3 What signs have you seen: (a) in school; (b) in an airport; (c) on doors; (d) at work; (e) outside?

4 Where have you seen notice boards? What kinds of things were on them?

5 Did you print or write the notes in this chapter? (It is acceptable to either print or write notes.) Could your partner read your handwriting?

6 Skim this chapter and circle all new vocabulary words. Make a list on the board of the vocabulary you remember from this chapter.

11

Business Letters

Teacher's Notes

Student Objectives:
- *to become familiar with the format of a business letter*
- *to become familiar with abbreviations commonly used in business letters*
- *to practice writing simple business letters for a variety of situations*

Sequence

1 Tell the class not to write anything until they have discussed each page.

2 The first three pages of this chapter deal with the form of a business letter. Use these pages as a preview for the chapter and have students refer back to them as they complete the rest of the chapter.

3 The next two pages in the chapter deal with abbreviations that can be used in business letters. Expand the lists of abbreviations by asking the students what other abbreviations they have seen. Ask the students to bring in business letters they have received. Look at them together. What abbreviations do you find in them?

4 The last six pages present models of business letters for different situations. Read each of the letters together. Then add vocabulary to the lists and fill in the blanks in the letters.

5 Complete the other exercises on the page.

Writing a Business Letter

1 WITH YOUR CLASS: Rules for Business Letter Writing

Look at the business letter on the next page. It follows the rules below. Read the rules with your class, using the letter on the next page as an example.

RULES FOR BUSINESS LETTER WRITING

1. Use 8½" × 11" white unlined paper.
2. Type or write on only one side of the paper.
3. Leave one inch margins at the top, bottom, and sides of the paper.
4. Type if you can. If you write, use black or dark blue ink.
5. Type your name after the closing. Leave enough space above your name for your handwritten signature.
6. Include all parts of the business letter:

   a. address of the sender
   b. dateline
   c. inside address
   d. salutation
   e. body of the letter
   f. closing
   g. signature

7. Fold the letter this way for a large envelope:

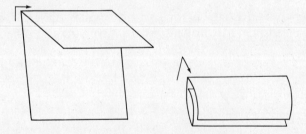

8. Fold the letter this way for a small envelope.

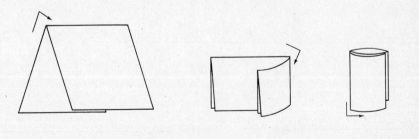

2 WITH YOUR CLASS: Identifying Parts of a Business Letter

Find more examples of the rules for business letter writing in other letters in this chapter.

_____

_____

_____

Consumer Information
Public Documents Distribution Center
Pueblo, Colorado 81009

Dear Sir or Madam:

Please send me a copy of your free booklet, Consumer Information. Thank you for your assistance.

Sincerely,

_____

Business Letter

1 WRITE YOUR OWN: Request for Consumer Information

Fill in the blanks on the business letter on the preceding page. Copy it on an 8½″ × 11″ piece of white paper. Fold it. Address and stamp an envelope. Mail the letter.

2 WITH YOUR CLASS: Consumer Information

With your class, read the consumer information listed below.

a. American Automotive Association (AAA). Look up the address in the telephone directory. Write for an application for membership.

b. The Parks and Recreation Division of your state. Look up the address in your telephone directory under your state name. Write to ask for a list of the public recreational facilities of your state.

c. U.S. Consumer Product Safety Commission, Washington, D.C. 20207. Ask for the latest publications.

d. The National Safety Council, 425 North Michigan Avenue, Chicago, Illinois 60611. Ask for a copy of the pamphlet, *Family Emergency Almanac.*

e. The Civil Aeronautics Board, Consumer Information Center, Pueblo, Colorado 81009. Ask for a copy of the pamphlet *Fly Rights* when you write the letter. It deals with passengers' rights on airlines.

3 WRITE YOUR OWN: Business Letter

On an 8½″ × 11″ piece of paper, write or type a business letter. Choose one of the possibilities listed above.

Common Abbreviations

1 ON THE BOARD: Acronyms

An *acronym* is a word formed from the first letter (or first few letters) of several words. Write the acronyms for the following. Then add to the list.

United Nations International Children's Emergency Fund _____

Oil Producing and Exporting Countries _____

Self-contained underwater breathing apparatus _____

other: _____

_____ _____

2 ON THE BOARD: Abbreviations

An *abbreviation* is a shortened form of a word or phrase. Write the abbreviations for the following words. Then add to the list.

Sunday _____		company _____	
Monday _____		department _____	
Tuesday _____		incorporated _____	
Wednesday _____		corporation _____	
Thursday _____		doctor _____	
Friday _____		January _____	
Saturday _____		February _____	
number _____		March _____	
page _____		April _____	
television _____		*other:* _____	

3 ON THE BOARD: Initials

An *initial* is the first letter of a word. Often initials are used to signify names of organizations, places, schools, etc. which have long names. Write the initials for the following. Then add to the list.

Central Intelligence Agency _____

Komitet Gosudarstvennoy Bezopastnosti (Committee for the Safety of the Country) _____

General Equivalency Diploma _____

Post office _____

other: _____

_____

_____

Using Abbreviations in Business Letters

1 WITH YOUR CLASS: Business Letters with Abbreviations

Read this business letter and discuss it with the class.

```
                                   415 Channing Rd.
                                   Burton, Pa.
                                   December 12, 1983

Main Office
State Div. of Employment
1400 Harding Street
Pittsburgh, Pa.

Attn:  Mr. James Polk

Dear Mr. Polk:

You sent me on a job interview to the Chas. T. Mann Co. one week
ago.  They gave me an aptitude test and a skills test.  Then they
hired me.

I want to express my appreciation to you for referring me to this
company.

                                   Yours truly,

                                   Joseph Blanchard

                                   Joseph Blanchard
```

2 ON THE BOARD: Abbreviations

Find the abbreviations in the letter above. Write them on the board. Write the long form for each abbreviation.

3 WITH YOUR CLASS: Other Abbreviations

What other company abbreviations do you know? With your class, make a list on the board.

4 WITH YOUR CLASS: Abbreviations of First Names

Complete this list of abbreviations of first names.

Charles   _____

Edward   _____

William   _____

Thomas   _____

_____   _____

_____   _____

_____   _____

Cover Letter For Returning a Purchase

Sometimes you may want to return an item you have bought. If the item is marked "satisfaction guaranteed" or if it has a warranty for a certain time period, the company must give you your money back. Send the item and also send a letter with the item explaining the problem—a cover letter.

1   WITH YOUR CLASS: Vocabulary

Read this cover letter with your class and add more words to the vocabulary list.

2   WRITE YOUR OWN: Cover Letter to Return a Purchase

Complete this cover letter.

```
_____
              (1)


_____
              (1)


_____
              (2)

General Merchandising, Inc.
Box 1400
Glendale, Arizona  55555

Dear Sir:

Last week I received the _____
                            (3)
I purchased from your company.  I am

_____ under separate
        (4)
cover because _____.
                    (5)

_____.
        (6)


_____
              (7)


_____
              (8)
```

1. *Your address*
2. *Today's date*
3. *Choose one:*
   - electric knife
   - clock
   - screwdriver set
   - *other:* _____
4. *Choose one:*
   - returning it
   - sending it back
5. *Choose one:*
   - it does not work
   - there are pieces missing
   - it was broken when I received it
   - I am not satisfied
   - *other:* _____
6. *Choose one:*
   - Please refund my money
   - Please send my money back
   - I would like a refund
   - *other:* _____
7. *Choose one:*
   - Yours truly
   - Sincerely
   - *other:* _____
8. *Your signature*

3   ON THE BOARD: Guaranteed Items

Make a list on the board of items that usually come with guarantees. If you have a written guarantee for an item, bring it to class. Share it with the other students.

Canceling a Subscription

When you want to stop your subscription to a magazine, a record club, or a book club, you must send a letter to the company.

1 WITH YOUR CLASS: Vocabulary

Read this letter with your class. Add more words to the vocabulary list.

2 WRITE YOUR OWN: Letter to Cancel a Subscription

Complete this letter.

_____ (1)

_____ (1)

_____ (2)

Subscription Department
Trans Com Media, Inc.
P.O. Box 7986
Columbia, MO 65205

Dear Sir or Madam:
      Please cancel my subscription.
I do not want to receive any more
_____ (3) . Since I

_____ (4)

please _____ (5)

_____ .

                    Sincerely yours,

_____ (6)

---

1. *Your address*
2. *The date*
3. *Choose one:*
   - newspapers
   - book selections
   - record selections
   - *other:* _____

     _____

4. *Choose one:*
   - have paid in advance
   - have returned the last selection
5. *Choose one:*
   - return the balance of the subscription payment
   - do not bill me
6. *Your signature*

Complaint—Billing Error

If you receive an incorrect bill, write a letter to the company. Explain the mistake and ask the company to correct it. Always make a copy of the bill and include it with the letter.

1 WITH YOUR CLASS: Vocabulary

Read this letter with your class and add more words to the vocabulary list.

2 WRITE YOUR OWN: Letter to Complain of a Billing Error

Complete this letter.

_____ (1)

_____ (1)

_____ (2)

ITL Company
Billing Department
Box 82
Danvers, Massachusetts 01923

Dear Sir or Madam:
    There is an error in the bill
I have just received. _____ (3)
_____.
(See enclosed copy of bill.) Please
investigate and correct this
situation.
              Yours truly,

_____ (4)

---

1. *Your address*
2. *Today's date*
3. *Choose one:*
   - I paid this bill last month
   - I did not purchase this item
   - You have billed me for the same item three times
   - I did not buy an alarm clock
   - I have written to you several times about this matter
4. *Your signature*

3 WRITE YOUR OWN: Billing Error Complaint to a Utility Company

Imagine you received a bill for $34.00 from the gas company. You have already paid the bill. Write a letter explaining the error.

Complaint to a Public Housing Agency

If you want to complain about your rental conditions, apartment maintenance, or safety hazards in your apartment or building, write to a local housing agency.

1 WITH YOUR CLASS: Vocabulary

Read this complaint letter with your class. Add more words to the vocabulary list.

2 WRITE YOUR OWN: Letter of Complaint

Complete this letter.

_____ (1)

_____ (1)

_____ (2)

_____ (3)

_____ (4)

_____ (4)

Dear Sir or Madam:

My landlord, _____ (5) , has

_____ (6) .

Please investigate this violation.

I appreciate your _____ (7)

this matter.

                    Sincerely,

_____ (8)

1. *Your address*
2. *Today's date*
3. *Your local agency*
4. *The address for line 3*
5. *Landlord's name*
6. *Choose one:*
   • not supplied sufficient heat
   • not fixed the broken elevator
   • raised the rent disregarding my lease
   • *other:* _____
   _____
   _____
7. *Choose one:*
   • help in
   • assistance in
   • immediate attention to
8. *Your signature*

3 WITH YOUR CLASS: Complaining by Telephone

You may want to call an agency and complain by telephone. Write a note to yourself to remember what to say when you call. Write down the following information:

1. the name of the agency you are calling

2. the telephone number of the agency you are calling

3. the landlord's name

4. the details. For example, if you are complaining about cockroaches, note the following:

   - how long the cockroaches have been in your apartment
   - where they are
   - the problems they cause
   - when you reported the problem to the superintendent
   - *other:* _____

   _____

College Admissions Request

Do you want to know more about a college or university? Write a letter requesting information.

1 WRITE YOUR OWN: Letter of Request

a. Go to your school counseling office or library and ask the counselor or librarian for the address of the college or university.

b. Fill in the choices in the letter below.

c. Write or type this letter on 8½″ × 11″ white paper.

d. When you receive an answer, bring it to class and share it.

```
                    _____
                          (1)
                    _____
                          (1)
                    _____
                          (2)

Admissions Officer

_____
        (3)
_____
        (4)
_____
        (4)

Dear Sir:

I am a _____ student at
             (5)
_____.  I am interested
        (6)
in applying for admission to your

_____ Program in
          (7)
_____.
        (8)
Would you please send me a catalogue,

an application for admission, financial aid

information and any other necessary forms.

        Sincerely,


        _____
                  (9)
```

1. *Your address*
2. *Today's date*
3. *Name of college*
4. *Address of college*
5. *Choose one:*
    - foreign
    - bilingual
6. *Name of your present school*
7. *Choose one:*
    - graduate
    - undergraduate
    - special
8. *Choose one:*
    - Liberal Arts
    - English as a Second Language
    - Engineering
    - *other:* _____
9. *Your signature*

CHAPTER FOLLOW-UP

1 What size margins should you use in a business letter?

2 What closings are appropriate for a business letter? Make a list of business letter closings on the board. Compare them to the closings on friendly letters, greeting cards, postcards, and telegrams.

3 What consumer information did you send for? Have you received it yet? Is it useful to you?

4 What is a cover letter? Look at Chapter 9, **Employment,** to see another kind of cover letter.

5 When would you make a complaint by:

    a. writing a business letter
    b. writing a note
    c. sending a telegram
    d. making a telephone call
    e. *other:* _____

6 Skim this chapter and circle all new vocabulary words. Make a list on the board of all the words you remember from this chapter.

Invitations

Teacher's Notes

Student Objective:
- *to become familiar with the common styles of written invitations, acceptances, and regrets in the United States.*

Sequence

1 Tell the students not to write anything before the class discusses the page.

2 To preview the chapter, skim the entire chapter, looking at the invitation model on each page. Talk about the differences between formal and informal, written and printed invitations.

3 To introduce each page with an invitation, provide a model of the invitation by reading it to the students, using the vocabulary from the list.

4 Ask the students when they have used written invitations in this country and for what occasions they used written or printed invitations in their native countries.

5 Have the students fill in the blanks. Make sure the choices fit together. (You can't write *on Saturday, October 31st* with *this summer*.)

6 Have the students complete the exercises on the page. Note that **Written Invitations, Letter of Acceptance,** and **Letter of Regret** should be completed as a unit, as should **Wedding Invitations, Acceptance,** and **Regret.**

Printed Fill-In Invitations

Card stores sell printed fill-in invitations for many occasions—birthday, anniversary, retirement, cocktail party, open house, and so on.

1 WITH A PARTNER: Birthday Party Invitation

Fill in the blanks on this birthday party invitation.

1. *A friend or relative's name*
2. *Choose one:*
   - 7:00 p.m.
   - seven o'clock
   - seven in the evening
3. *Choose one:*
   - November 19
   - November 19th
   - Nov. 19
   - 11/19
   - *other:* _____
4. *Your address*
5. *Your name*
6. *Your telephone number*

2 ON THE BOARD: Open House Invitation

On the board, draw an invitation form. Use it to write an invitation to other students for an open house at your home.

Handwritten Invitations

1 WITH A PARTNER: Writing an Invitation
Complete this written invitation to your partner.

_(1)_

Dear _____ ,
_(2)_

_____ _to_
_(3)_

_____
_(4)_

_____
_(5)_

_____ .
_(6)_

Please _____ .
_(7)_

Sincerely,

_____
_(8)_

1. *Today's date*
2. *Your partner's name*
3. *Choose one:*
   - You're invited
   - Please come
   - I would be pleased if you could come
   - I'd like to invite you
4. *Choose one:*
   - a New Year's Eve party
   - have dinner with us
   - a dinner party
   - a shower
   - visit me
   - *other:* _____
     _____
     _____
5. *Choose one:*
   - on your vacation
   - on Saturday, October 31st
   - *other:* _____
     _____
     _____
6. *Choose one:*
   - this summer
   - next month
   - at 8:00 p.m.
   - *other:* _____
     _____
     _____
7. *Choose one:*
   - give me a call.
   - let me know if you can come.
8. *Your signature*

2 WITH A PARTNER: Exchanging Invitations
Exchange your invitation with your partner. Answer with an acceptance or a regret.

Letter of Acceptance

Answer "yes" to an invitation with a letter of acceptance.

1 WITH A PARTNER: Writing a Letter of Acceptance

Write a letter of acceptance to your partner's invitation.

_____
(1)

Dear _____,
(2)
    Thank you for inviting

me _____.
(3)

I _____.
(4)

I'm looking forward to

seeing you then.

Sincerely,

_____
(5)

1. *Date*
2. *Your partner's name*
3. *Choose one:*
   - to visit you
   - to dinner
   - to the shower
   - to your open house
   - *other:* _____
     _____
     _____
4. *Choose one:*
   - am so glad I can come
   - would love to come
   - would like to come
   - accept your invitation gladly
   - am delighted to accept
5. *Your signature*

Letter of Regret

1   WITH A PARTNER: Writing a Letter of Regret
Write a letter of regret to your partner's invitation.

_____
(1)

Dear _____ ,
(2)
Thank you for inviting
me _____
(3)
_____ .

_____
(4)
I won't be able to _____
(5)
_____
because _____
(6)
_____ .

Sincerely,

_____
(7)

1. *Today's date*
2. *Your partner's name*
3. *Choose one:*
   - to stay with you
   - to your party
   - for the weekend
   - *other:* _____
   _____
   _____
4. *Choose one:*
   - Unfortunately
   - I'm sorry that
   - I'm disappointed that
5. *Choose one:*
   - accept
   - come
   - be there
   - be with you
6. *Choose one:*
   - I have a previous engagement
   - I'm going to be away
   - I'm sick with the flu
   - I have to work
7. *Your signature*

Wedding Invitations

A formal wedding invitation may look like this:

Mr. and Mrs. Joseph J. Zajac
request the honour of your presence
at the marriage of their daughter
Maria Jolanta
to
Mr. Steven S. Skoropowski
on Sunday, the twenty-seventh of April
nineteen hundred and eighty
at two o'clock
Holy Trinity Church
340 High Street
Lowell, Massachusetts

1   WRITE YOUR OWN: Response Card

Many people include a reception card and a response card with the wedding invitation. Fill in the response card for this wedding.

Reception

at three o'clock

Nat Sergi's Joseph's Lounge

Lowell, Massachusetts

Please respond on or before

April 11th, 1980

M. _____

will _____ attend

will not _____ attend

Wedding Acceptance and Regret

1 WRITE YOUR OWN: Letter of Acceptance
Complete this letter of acceptance.

_____(1)_____ _____(2)_____

_____ *with pleasure*
(3)
Mr. and Mrs. Joseph J. Zajec's
kind invitation for
Sunday, the twenty-seventh of April
at two o'clock

1. *Choose one:*
   - Miss
   - Ms.
   - Mrs.
   - Mr.
   - Mr. and Mrs.
2. *Your name*
3. *Choose one:*
   - accept
   - accepts

2 WRITE YOUR OWN: Letter of Regret
Complete this letter of regret.

_____(1)_____ _____(2)_____

_____ *unable to accept*
(3)
Mr. and Mrs. Joseph J. Zajec's
kind invitation for
Sunday, the twenty-seventh of April

1. *Choose one:*
   - Mr.
   - Mrs.
   - Ms.
   - Mr. and Mrs.
2. *Your name*
3. *Choose one:*
   - regrets that she is
   - regrets that he is
   - regret that they are

13

Announcements

Teacher's Notes

Student Objective:
- *to become familiar with the common styles of newspaper announcements and telegrams*

Sequence

1   Tell the students not to write anything until the class has discussed the page.

2   To preview this chapter, skim the entire chapter, looking at the illustrations on each page. Talk about the kinds of announcements you find in a newspaper and the kinds of telegrams you send and receive.

3   With the class, read through the newspaper clippings of each announcement, telegram, and mailgram. Discuss the vocabulary on each page.

4   Ask the students how the events on each page are announced in their native countries.

5   Complete all the exercises on the pages.

Birth Announcement

When a baby is born, many hospitals give a Birth Statement to the mother. She may fill it in and send it to the local newspaper if she wishes.

1 WITH YOUR CLASS: Birth Announcement
Study the birth announcements in this newspaper clipping. Choose one announcement and find the following information:

1. Names of the parents _____
2. Address of the parents _____
3. Sex of the baby _____
4. Date of birth _____
5. Place of birth _____
6. Names of the grandparents _____
7. City, town or country where the grandparents live _____

Births

Mr. and Mrs. Jose A. Sanchez, of 929 Haverhill street, Rowley, announce the birth of their son, Andrew James, on April 9 at Hunt Memorial Hospital. Mrs. Sanchez is the former Nadine Griffin, of Danvers. Grandparents are Mr. and Mrs. James R. Griffin, of Rowley, and Mr. Jose Sanchez, of the Dominican Republic.

* * *

Mr. and Mrs. Edward J. Lynch, Jr. of 38 Riverside street, announce the birth of their daughter, Elizabeth Irene, on April 7, at Salem Hospital. Grandparents are Mr. and Mrs. Edward Lynch, Sr., of Danvers, and Mr. and Mrs. Raymond MacNeil, also of Danvers. Great-grandmother is Mrs. Elton MacNeil, of Peabody.

* * *

Mr. and Mrs. Richard Crozdowicz, of 66 Wenham street, announce the birth of their son, Brian Richard, on April 6 at Salem Hospital. Grandparents are Mr. and Mrs. Kenneth Taylor, of Marblehead, and Mr. and Mrs. Henry Drozdowicz, of Saugus.

2 WRITE YOUR OWN: Writing a Birth Announcement
Write a birth announcement for yourself or for one of your children. Include all the necessary information.

Birth announcement courtesy of the *Danvers Herald,* Danvers, Mass.

Telegram to Notify of a Birth

1 WITH YOUR CLASS: Writing a Telegram

Pretend that another student in your class just had a baby (or some babies). Write a telegram to the student's family to notify them of the "blessed event."

Telegram — western union

MSG. NO.	NO. WDS CL. OF SVC.	PD.—COLL.	CASH NO.	ACCOUNTING INFORMATION	DATE	FILING TIME	SENT TIME
						A.M. / P.M.	A.M. / P.M.

SEND THE FOLLOWING MESSAGE, SUBJECT TO THE TERMS ON BACK HEREOF, WHICH ARE HEREBY AGREED TO.

☐ OVERNIGHT TELEGRAM
UNLESS BOX ABOVE IS CHECKED THIS MESSAGE WILL BE SENT AS A TELEGRAM.

(1) TO _____ CARE OF OR APARTMENT NO. _____

ADDRESS & TELEPHONE NO. _____

CITY — STATE & ZIP CODE _____

(2) _____
(3) _____
(4) _____
(5) _____
(6) _____

(7) SENDER'S TEL. NO. _____ NAME & ADDRESS _____

OFFICE USE ONLY

EOM (_____ / _____ / _____ / _____ / _____)
(BILL TO)   (ADDRESS)   (CITY - STATE - ZIP)   (CHG. METH.) X-OFF
_____ / _____ / _____ / _____ / _____ / _____ / _____ / _____
(CHG.#) (OPR.#) (HF) (PC CODE) (PC AMT.) (GIFT AMT.) (TAX) (AGT. I.D.) (SG)

1. *Write the name and address of another student's relative.*
2. *Choose one:*
   - You're a grandma!
   - You're a grandpa!
   - You're an aunt!
   - You're an uncle!
   - You're a father!
3. *Choose one:*
   - It's a boy!
   - It's a girl!
   - Twins!
   - Triplets!
   - Quadruplets!
   - Quintuplets!
   - Sextuplets!
4. *Choose one:*
   - Midnight
   - 3:00 a.m.
   - Noon
   - 4:27 p.m.
5. *Choose one:*
   - 6 lbs. 11 oz.
   - 4 lbs. 2 oz.
   - 2 boys, 1 girl.
   - 4 boys
   - 3 girls, 2 boys
   - 6 girls.
6. *Choose one:*
   - Mother and baby doing fine.
   - Mother and babies healthy.
   - Babies premature but all are well.
7. *Your telephone number, name and address*

Death Notice (Obituary)

When someone dies, the funeral home sends a short death notice to the local newspaper. Often the person's family also places a longer death announcement in the newspaper. A death notice is also called an *obituary*.

1 WITH YOUR CLASS: Obituaries

Compare these two death announcements and answer the questions below.

DEATHS

BACIGALUPO — In Biddeford, Maine, April 10, 1980, Mr. John Bacigalupo, a resident of 74 Chadwick Street, Bradford. In his 99th year. Widower of Annie (Cassola) Bacigulapo, father of John L. Bacigalupo of Kennebunkport, Maine, of Mrs. Arthur (Virginia) Clockadale of Orlando, Florida and Mrs. Norma Angelotti of Haverhill. A private funeral will be held. At the request of the family there will be no calling hours. Funeral arrangements are by the Scatamacchia & D'Amico Funeral Home, 358 Washington Street, Haverhill.

Deaths

John Bacigalupo, Johnny's Oil founder

John Bacigalupo, 99, of 74 Chadwick St., died Thursday at the home of his son in Kennebunkport, Maine.

He was the founder of Johnny's Oil Co.

He was born in Genoa, Italy, Jan. 27, 1881, son of the late Giuseppe and Rose (Debardieri) Bacigalupo.

He was a resident of this country for more than 70 years.

He owned and operated Johnny's Oil Co. with his son until his retirement in 1964.

He attended Sacred Hearts Church and was a life member of the Haverhill Lodge of Elks.

He was the widower of Annie (Cassola) Bacigalupo.

He leaves his son, John L., Kennebunkport, Maine; two daughters, Mrs. Norma Angelotti, Haverhill, and Mrs. Arthur (Virginia) Clockedale, Orlando, Fla.; nine grandchildren; 15 great-grandchildren; and several nieces and nephews.

A private funeral will be held.

At the request of the family, there will be no calling hours. Burial will be in Elmwood Cemetery.

Funeral arrangements are by Scatamacchia and D'Amico Funeral Home, 358 Washington St.

Questions:

1. Which announcement did the funeral home give to the newspaper?

2. Which announcement did Mr. Bacigalupo's family write?

3. What additional information is included in the longer announcement?

2 WITH YOUR CLASS: Death Notices in Your Native Country

When someone dies in your native country, does the local newspaper announce the death? Does a death notice contain the same information in your native country?

Obituary courtesy of the *Haverhill Gazette*, Haverhill, Mass.

Telegram or Mailgram to Notify of a Death

People often send either a telegram or a mailgram to notify relatives and friends of a death. A mailgram costs less than a telegram and travels more slowly. You may write fifty words in a mailgram. The name and address are included in the fifty words. More than fifty words costs extra.

1 **WITH YOUR CLASS:** Change a Mailgram to a Telegram.

Copy the fifteen underlined words in the mailgram below to make a telegram message.

Sending Blank   western union **Mailgram**   UNITED STATES POSTAL SERVICE · U.S. MAIL

ADDRESSEE'S NAME MRS. DIANE MILLER ADDRESSEE'S FIRM (IF APPLICABLE)	DATE
STREET ADDRESS 2 FOREST LANE CITY, STATE AND ZIP CODE MILTON, PENNSYLVANIA	

MESSAGE: I'M SO SORRY TO TELL YOU THAT <u>GIL DUPONT</u> HAS DIED. HE <u>HAD A SUDDEN</u>

<u>HEART ATTACK</u> ON <u>MONDAY</u> MORNING, OCTOBER 28. WE TOOK HIM TO THE

HOSPITAL, BUT HE <u>DIED</u> THERE ON <u>TUESDAY</u> OCTOBER 29. THE <u>FUNERAL</u>

WILL BE HELD FRIDAY, <u>NOVEMBER 1</u>, AT 2:00 IN THE AFTERNOON. IT WILL BE

AT LARRON'S FUNERAL HOME, HERE IN <u>SPRINGFIELD</u>.

SENDER'S NAME (PLEASE PRINT) HIRO KATSUNUMA	SENDER'S SIGNATURE
SENDER'S ADDRESS & ZIP CODE 22 PROSPECT DRIVE, SPRINGFIELD, ILLINOIS	TELEPHONE NO./AREA CODE

---

western union   **Telegram**

Forms courtesy of Western Union Telegraph Co.

Engagement Announcement

Your local newspaper will publish announcements of graduations, engagements, weddings, or any local social event. If you send in the information, the newspaper reporters will write the story. Include your telephone number and address. Send a black and white photo if you want the picture included.

1 WITH YOUR CLASS: Engagement Announcement

Read the newspaper engagement announcement. Find the following information:

Gonsalves-Ingalls

Mr. and Mrs. Joseph Gonsalves, 12 Nelson Ave., Georgetown, Mass., announce the engagement of their daughter, Lynne Anne Gonsalves, to Robert Ingalls, son of Mr. and Mrs. Norman Ingalls, 1 Middle Road, Amesbury.

Miss Gonsalves is a hostess at Sawyer's Restaurant.

Her fiance attended Haverhill Trade School and is employed by Haverhill Tool Co.

They plan to marry June 14.

Lynne Anne Gonsalves

1. *Name of the parents of the engaged couple*

_____

2. *Names of the engaged couple*

_____

3. *Education of the engaged couple*

_____

4. *Employment of the engaged couple*

_____

5. *Date of the wedding*

_____

2 WITH YOUR CLASS: More Engagement Announcements

Bring in a page of engagement announcements from a local newspaper. Look at the announcements and compare them to the one above. Do they have the same information? What is different?

3 ON THE BOARD: Write an Engagement Announcement

Is anyone in your class engaged or married? On the board, write the necessary information (see Exercise 1) for an engagement announcement for that student. Then write the announcement.

Engagement announcement courtesy of the *Haverhill Gazette,* Haverhill, Mass.

Wedding Announcement

To announce a wedding in your local newspaper, write a letter like this and send it with a black and white wedding photograph.

1   WITH YOUR CLASS: Announcing a Wedding in the Newspaper

Read this letter to a newspaper and the newspaper announcement of the wedding. How are weddings announced in your native country?

12 Exeter St.
Boston, Mass. 02120
April 5, 1980

Boston Globe
Announcements
Boston, Mass. 02120

Dear Sirs:

Would you please print this wedding announcement?

Ming Hoang Thi Chau, of Vietnam, and Phuc Dac Ta, of Hanover, were married in Abington. The bride is the daughter of Mr. and Mrs. Quang Minh Chau, and attended Can Tho University. The bridegroom is the son of Mr. and Mrs. Vong Dac Ta, and is attending Northeastern University. The couple is living in Boston, following a trip to Washington.

I have enclosed a 3"x 5" black and white photograph. The wedding took place on March 20. My phone number is 641-2078.

Thank you very much.

Sincerely,
Mrs. Phuc Dac Ta

Dac Ta / Chau

Mr. and Mrs. Phuc Dac Ta

Minh Hoang Thi Chau, Vietnam, and Phuc Dac Ta, Hanover, were married in Abington. The bride, daughter of Mr. and Mrs. Quang Minh Chau, attended Can Tho University. The bridegroom, son of Mr. and Mrs. Vong Dac Ta, is attending Northeastern University. The couple is living in Boston, following a trip to Washington.

Wedding announcement courtesy of *The Boston Globe*.

2 WRITE YOUR OWN: Writing a Letter for a Wedding Announcement

Complete this letter to your local newspaper for your own wedding or for the wedding of someone you know. (*Note:* Follow the rules for business letter writing.)

1. Your address
2. Today's date
3. Name of the newpaper
4. Announcement Department
5. Address of the newspaper
6. Name of the bride
7. Name of the groom
8. Place of the wedding
9. Name of bride's parents
10. Name of groom's parents
11. City or town where the couple will live
12. Date of wedding
13. Your phone number
14. Your signature

_____ (1)
_____
_____ (2)

_____ (3)
_____ (4)
_____ (5)
_____

Dear Sir or Madam:
   Would you please print this announcement?_____
_____ and (6)
_____ (7)
were married at _____. The
bride is the daughter of _____ (8) _____ (9). The
bridegroom is the son of _____ (10) _____. The
couple will live in _____ (11).
   I have enclosed a 3"x5" black and white photo. The wedding took place on _____.
My phone number is _____ (12) _____.
Thank you very much. (13)
   Sincerely,

_____ (14)

Wedding Anniversary Announcement

People often announce twenty-fifth and fiftieth wedding anniversaries in the newspaper. The announcement may include a photograph.

1 WITH YOUR CLASS: Silver and Golden Anniversaries

When a couple has been married twenty-five years, they celebrate their *silver anniversary*. When a couple has been married fifty years, they celebrate their *golden anniversary*. Their family often gives a special party.

Read the golden and silver anniversary announcements on the opposite page.

Is there a similar custom in your native country? Discuss this with the class.

2 ON THE BOARD: Write an Anniversary Announcement

Does anyone in your class have relatives who have been married twenty-five or fifty years? Write an announcement on the board for their silver or golden anniversary.

Mr. and Mrs. John J. Cahill

Wed 50 years

Mr. and Mrs. John J. Cahill of Sarasota, Fla., formerly of Haverhill, recently observed their 50th wedding anniversary at an open house, November 4th, at the home of their daughter, Mrs. Joseph (Shirley) St. Germain of Groveland.

The open house was also given by their other children and their spouses, Mr. and Mrs. John F. Cahill, Mr. and Mrs. Michael (Dianne) Connolly and Mr. and Mrs. Thomas (Mary Ellen) Dooley.

The coupe was married on Oct. 26, 1929 in St. James Church by the Rev. Joseph O'Toole.

Their attendants were Mr. and Mrs. Albert Paquette. Mrs. Paquette was present at the golden wedding observance.

The Cahill's have eight grandchildren.

Silver anniversary

AMESBURY — Mr. and Mrs. Frank Gruber, 24 Collins St., were honored on their 25th wedding anniversary with a party Jan. 5 in the Polish Club, Mill St.

They were married Jan. 1, 1955 in St. Michael's Church, Haverhill.

Among those attending were Mr. and Mrs. Joseph Jezierski, Methuen, best man and maid of honor.

Other guests attended from Amesbury, Lawrence, Lowell and Portsmouth, N.H.

The couple received many cards, gifts, flowers and money.

A catered dinner was served the nearly 100 persons present. An anniversary cake was cut and served.

GOLDEN ANNIVERSARIES

Mr. and Mrs. Joseph T. Cotone, 42 Dale rd., Holbrook; 50 years on April 5; married in South Boston. Three children, 15 grandchildren and four great-grandchildren.

Mr. and Mrs. Anthony Ruggiero, 147A Brandywyne dr., East Boston; 50 years on April 26; married in East Boston. Two children and four grandchildren.

Anniversary announcements courtesy of the *Haverhill Gazette*, Haverhill, Mass.

CHAPTER FOLLOW-UP

1 Do newspaper announcements of births, engagements, weddings, and deaths in your country look like the ones in this chapter? If not, how are they different?

2 Did you ever receive a telegram or mailgram announcement? What was it for? Did you ever send one?

3 Sometimes new parents announce the birth of their baby by sending printed fill-in announcement cards. Where can you buy announcement cards in your community? What other personal events can be announced in this way?

4 Clubs and other social groups often announce events using posters or flyers. What are posters and flyers? Where do you see them?

Index of Tasks and Themes in Everyday Writing